THE INSECT GARDEN

The Best Plants For Bees & Bumblebees, Butterflies, Hoverflies & Other Insects

Michael John Seabrook

Save Our Insects!

Northern Bee Books

All photographs taken by Michael John Seabrook Copyright 2020

Thank you to Jeremy Burbidge for seeing the opportunity of this book and to David Miller for perseverance through a complex project.

ISBN 978-1-912271-55-9

Published by Northern Bee Books, 2020
Scout Bottom Farm
Mytholmroyd
Hebden Bridge HX7 5JS (UK)

Design and artwork by DM Design and Print

THE INSECT GARDEN

The Best Plants For Bees & Bumblebees, Butterflies, Hoverflies & Other Insects

Michael John Seabrook

Save Our Insects!

Dedicated to John and Dorothy Seabrook – with love

CONTENTS

PREFACE

In the UK we are building more and more houses with smaller and smaller gardens. Environmental spaces are being swallowed up in order for concrete to be King. Larger back gardens are having houses planted within them leading to the reduction of green spaces. Farmland now has giant fields with very significant loss of available habitat such as hedgerows.

At the same time we have had a catastrophic decrease in the number of insects, birds and other animals (*as described in Chapter 1*). This is a disaster, and one that gets overlooked, too often in my view. If our population of humans had declined by **billions** would that not be on the news, every single day? Some of our most common and valuable trees are also under threat of disease and set to decline and this also seriously affects insects, birds and bats among others (*see Chapter 7*).

However, small spaces we *can* provide for wildlife in our gardens become more and more valuable. The plants that bees, butterflies and other insects visit for pollen and nectar provide them with food. A healthy ecological base can be established which benefits birds and other creatures. This could reverse insect decline.

This book looks at how to select and grow the best plants to create a wildlife *beneficial* garden. It includes the results of my research over more than 20 years to make sure that every plant you put in your garden makes the maximum contribution for insects. There is a huge difference in how good plants are for them which is why every one, good or bad, has a score between 0 and 150. *Chapters 4, 5, 6, 7, 10, 12 and the Appendix* explore the results of my research. You can be living in town, or in the country, the selected plants will work hard to support your local insect population.

Conversely, and In a special feature, I warn against plants, often found in garden centres (and gardens) that can actually KILL bees. You can help bee populations by removing, or not growing these.

I'll also give you planting plans and designs (*Chapter 12*) for "*Concentrated Ecology Planting*". These range from a hanging basket to a "hot bed" perennial border. In *Chapters 8 and 9* I provide information on how bees operate their unique society, moving on to plant associations with butterflies, moths and hoverflies. I give hints on "Season Stretchers" *(Chapter 6)* plants that will flower later in the season to help insects that are then about, to combat the effect of warming climate.

Finally I will be challenging at times within these chapters. I'm not here to write a boring (or traditional) gardening book! If this does not disturb you then read on, because we can help **save our insects**, whilst making our gardens beautiful, for all of us, too.

Michael John Seabrook December 2019

CHAPTER 1 - WHY INSECTS NEED OUR HELP

This book does focus on pollinating insects. By this I mean all types of bees, bumblebees, solitary bees, hoverflies, butterflies and to a limited extent other insects. This is my attempt (in however a small way) to try to help maintain or increase the populations of them by encouraging the planting of the right plants to feed them (with pollen or nectar) in our gardens.

Insects are at the bottom of the food chain. The bottom is actually more important than the top. Without the bottom, the top will not exist! I want you to (now) imagine who you think is top of the food chain? I'll come back to this later...

Those of us who don't, must learn to love the "bugs", the funny or "ugly "insects. They support the more "cute" creatures we all love by providing them with food. Nobody wants to hug a hoverfly. But if you ever look closely at a hoverfly, or a bumblebee, well most of them are *beautiful* creatures. I feel that every type of creature has its place, in the natural order or balance and it has the right to exist.

The population decreases in the UK of all animals, including insects, make grim reading. There are no pretty pictures in this book for a while, if there were they would be of billions of small, dead, creatures. But you need facts, to show you why there is a problem and why we need to do something about it. So I'm going to give you those and then show you how we can help this situation.

Insects could vanish within a century at current rate of decline, says global review
(Reported in the Guardian 10/02/19)

Insects and other invertebrates that make up 97 per cent of all animal species are struggling, with 75 per cent in decline over the past 25 years in the UK
(Reported in the Guardian 18/10/17)

Krefeld Entomological Society in Germany was one of the first studies to show this phenomenon, now seen as worldwide. **The catch of insects in test areas had fallen by nearly 80% in 2013 across a dozen sites** (sciencemag.org) and populations have continued to fall.The mass of insects collected by monitoring traps in the Orbroicher Bruch Nature reserve in Northwest Germany **dropped by 78% in 24 years**. But if you have been on this planet for a while, you will KNOW insects have decreased it is OBVIOUS. I remember dozens of bees in one garden, 20 years ago, jostling one another to feed on their favourite plants. No longer. The thing is for younger people to realise the much smaller insect population we have now is **not** normality.

Around 80% of plants rely on insects for pollination, and birds gobble them (or caterpillars that would turn into insects) for sustenance. But we use pesticides on our potential food, and these kill beneficial as well as supposedly non beneficial insects. And who eats the pears, that were covered in pesticides, that killed all the bees as is now happening? It is us, the top of the food chain. We are eating the very things that have helped kill insects. Why would we be totally immune to deadly poison that kills other creatures? Just think about that for a while.

And it is not just insects. **There are less than 1 million hedgehogs estimated to be in the UK as I write this. In the 1950's there was estimated to be over 30 million**. (Source BTO) What would happen if the human population had such a reverse in the last 70 years?

Among the worst hit bird species are **house sparrows that have declined by around 150 million birds in the past 30 years. Starlings have seen their numbers fall by 45 million.** (source BTO)

An annual survey showed a **"steady decline" in the bee sourced honey crop.** The British Beekeepers Association (BBKA) said that beekeepers in England produced an average of 11.8kg (26 lb) of honey per hive year. (as reported in the Guardian and elsewhere Oct 2018)

Long-time beekeepers tell us that a crop of 25-45kg was typical in the 1950s.In the USA, there were 6 million Bee colonies in 1960, and just over 2 million now.

And we should listen to our Beekeepers when they say that Pesticides, including Neonicotinoids, were linked to this decline. Traces of the pesticide are increasingly found in honey, (which proves the pesticide is actually IN bees as honey is made within their bodies) 75% of honey, everywhere except Antartica, has a trace of pesticide within it. (as reported by Nature.Com from article in Science Magazine)

Widely used insecticides were shown to damage the survival of honeybee colonies in a very large field trial completed in 2018. Harm is also caused to all other bee species. The report suggested widespread contamination of entire landscapes and a toxic "cocktail effect" from multiple pesticides. (source "Science" Journal)

Neonicotinoids are synthetic versions of nicotine. These make up a quarter of the multi-billion dollar pesticide market but have been repeatedly linked to serious harm in bees in lab-based studies.

"They attack the brain of the insect, causing paralysis and death, and at lower doses interfere with navigation, disease resistance and learning. They are remarkably toxic to insects. Just four-billionths of a gram is a lethal dose to a honey bee, meaning one teaspoon of neonics is enough to give a lethal dose to one and a quarter billion bees.

Neonics work systemically in plants and can be sprayed onto leaves, watered into the soil, or used as a seed coating. Whatever route is used, they end up throughout the tissues of a plant, including in its sap, nectar and pollen. They are also highly persistent; once in the soil they remain there for years." Professor Dave Goulson Friends of the Earth

But this is not all that bees are concerned with.   A third of beekeepers feared the loss of forage from agricultural development, 28% were worried about varroa mite pests, others had concerns about the invasive and voracious Asian Hornet which preys on honeybees (already reported in South East England in 2019) and many others were anxious about the effects of climate change.

This is quite a serious in-tray for the future of the honey bee and that transfers to all other types of bee too. But why are they important to us Humans? Why should we care about bees and other pollinators?

Sources such as the University of Reading (adopted by Government) stated that insect pollinators added £691 million per year in 2014 to the value of the UK economy through yield achieved by the pollination provided. Applying appropriate inflation increases the figure to around £800 million for 2020. The quality of various fruit and vegetables also depends on the bee. All types of bee including bumblebees and solitary bees are very effective pollinators. If bees get fewer, we have less food, of a poorer quality, and it will be much more expensive. Does any of this sound like a good idea? At the extremes of this scenario, with no insects at all we have hardly any food. What happens then? We starve, simply put.

Climate change where it produces milder Winters is harmful for butterflies because of the increased rate of diseases, predation and the disruption of overWintering behaviour. Butterflies or caterpillars may also emerge from Winter hibernation too early and then are being killed when cold weather returns. In fact 2018 had this with a late, very cold Winter in March with nature delayed by a month, with the hope it would catch up. Cold Springs are harmful as the ability of butterflies to fly is hampered, meaning the earlier ones cannot breed and lay eggs.

Drought is a disaster for any butterfly or moth seeking a food plant that is otherwise dried up and will not feed a caterpillar. Butterflies have a finite life, often only about 20 days, so they may die in a drought without reproducing.

Blue tits and blackbirds are a good example of birds very much affected by the weather. For a pair of blue tits to succeed in raising a brood, they need a plentiful supply of moth caterpillars. The best caterpillar 'crops' are available in years when the Spring is warm and sunny with low rainfall, and the tits' breeding success is correspondingly high (source RSPB)

Pesticides, hedgerows being ripped up and the intensification of farming have contributed to a 55 per cent fall in farmland birds since 1970. And to add to this grim chapter, the decline in the once "common" Frog, and Toads and Newts, and the decline of Slow worm populations, the absence of Swifts last Summer for the first time where I live, the steep decline of Bats (who only eat insects).

The "causes" of the decline in all animal species as well as insects include the intensification of farming, with the consequent loss of meadows, hedgerows and ponds and increased pesticide use, as well as building development, overfishing and climate change. Three in every five of the 3,148 species analysed for the State of Nature report 2013 have declined in the last 50 years and one in 10 are at risk of extinction. And that was 2014. It continues to get much worse.

Are you putting together pieces of a jigsaw puzzle here? Every single problem outlined in this chapter does go back to the reduction in the number of insects.

Everything in nature is interconnected, one way or another, it is all facing a huge crisis and we are top of the food chain, this connection, is to us.

Bees have already faced severe reductions in numbers where over-extensive farming contributes to a loss in natural bee habitat. Pesticides can kill them all off. Commercial bees are then introduced into an area to fill in for the indigenous bees, but due to the pesticides, they then may all die. Human pollination can be used, but this is less than half as effective as insect pollination. Yields are vastly decreased. Food became scarce. If this is our future, is this not staring down the barrel of a gun?

I can't believe that the cause of declining animal and insect populations is something us humans are immune from forever. The last paragraph is one example. but, If everything else is dying off in this world, how can we **not** be affected?

What about the increase in cancer, now at a rate of one person in two in the UK? Think about the increase in other diseases. Look at our children who suffer all sorts of allergic reactions to food. In just three decades this has gone from rare, to very common. Are we, all of us, a great "experiment" where the conclusion comes too late for all of us? I'm not having a go at farmers here. It is the responsibility of us all to find a different way of doing things, to respect the environment and that includes looking for solutions that do not involve a soup of dozens of different deadly chemicals applied to our crop fields with such a catastrophic effect on biodiversity.

So we need to support insects, not just by planting "wildlife plants" which provide forage, pollen and nectar for them. But we have to plant the best plants, at the best time of year, and concentrate any wildlife garden to best use the space. The good news is that these plant choices are also the best for making a colourful, beautiful garden.

This is what I call, Concentrated **Ecology Gardening.** But this is more than just words! There is a description and rationale behind these two words which I outline in the next chapter.

CONCLUDING WORDS

So let us finish on a positive note. If you want to help insect populations, you are in the right place!

There is enough choice of plants in this book to cater for any personal taste in plants to make your garden one that supports and nurtures insects.

Whilst we still have honey bees, bumblebees, solitary bees, hoverflies, butterflies and moths we can help their populations to bounce back whilst there are still enough of them to do so. But we must act now. Read on, and find out how...

CHAPTER 2 - PRINCIPLES OF PLANT SELECTION

Thank you for getting through the tough first chapter of my book. Things get more positive from here on.

I knew someone who told me proudly she had a "wildlife friendly garden" as it was full of weeds and completely overgrown. Wildlife will not judge an untidy garden as a negative thing. A wildlife garden can be tidy or formal or informal. Mine (pictured above) is somewhere between. The key to a successful wildlife garden is the plants that are used and how well they grow. This is especially true when wanting to attract insects such as bees, bumblebees butterflies and hoverflies. In this book the theory of **Ecology Gardening** will make a real difference to your local pollinating insects versus any other traditional way of gardening or choosing plants. Here is my set of logical and easy rules to follow.

RULE 1 ONLY THE BEST WILDLIFE BENEFICIAL PLANTS TO BE PLANTED

From my research I developed a method of scoring individual plants which I developed over many years. This method is explained in Chapter 3 with the full results in the separate appendix. I found a wide difference between plants that did attract bees butterflies and hoverflies and those that didn't. So that leads me to this first rule. There are plants that really help insects and many others that will do nothing, or relatively not much. My scores go from 0 to 150 which reflect this fact.

Many bedding plants such as Pelagonium are less useful than a cardboard box to insects. The same for double flowered perennials. So this rule says in summary.

JUST plant the plants that really help for a wildlife garden. Don't plant any other plants. Gradually lose those in your gardens that have little value to insects.

This book recommends the best plants, and they are a real variety of plant types, shapes, sizes and colours. There is something for everyone here!

RULE 2 - NO "DIVA" PLANTS

I just use this term for plants that need rather a lot of fuss. This can include half hardy plants or frost hardy plants, which you may need to pamper to get through the Winter. This can mean those that are difficult to grow, though these can , of course, be very good for insects.

But they can also be a waste of valuable time.   I'm going to assume you want to spend the smallest time possible with your insect border wanting the best result. And in that context a failed plant will cost you money to replace, and a dead plant or struggling plant will not help the insects. It will not flower sufficiently to benefit them.

The amount of effort you put in will often equal the reward so I do include some "Diva" plants where they scored well for insects. But if you have too many other things in your life, then in the appendix and elsewhere I point out the pros and cons of certain plants and the relative attention they need! It is a choice.

RULE 3 - NO PLANTS FOR A SLUGS BREAKFAST

As any gardener knows, there are plants that are loved (and thus can be totally destroyed) by slugs. Anybody who has bought a plant for £8 at a Garden Centre and seen it munched by a "cornucopia" of slugs (they are never without friends) a few days later will wonder about the logic of having bought the plant in the first place! Often plants will have leaves eaten to the base, without hope of recovery.

Every year in the UK millions of pounds are spent by us to control slugs on plants we buy that are vulnerable to slugs! Horrible chemicals are poured onto our gardens, causing death to birds if they eat metaldehyde pellets. I have a simple solution to this problem which will save you money and trouble.

BUY PLANTS THAT SLUGS ARE LESS LIKELY TO EAT.

This may seem defeatist but it isn't. If you want success in your garden and have limited time, and if you don't have a pond (see chapter 10) then you could waste time and money on plants whereas other options will work better for you. I have a conflict here with my own rule as this book is here to identify the best insect plants. So I identify slug vulnerable plants that you may choose to avoid and therefore make other choices. If you have a pond this will most likely have frogs and toads to eat at least *some* of the slugs in a given area.

There are "friendly" ways of killing slugs such as putting cheap beer in a submerged cup at soil level. The slugs basically get dead-drunk and you are left with a fizzy, slimy, yucky, slug-beer to dispose of. I prefer gravel around plants or "preventative" methods none of which always totally work but do help a bit. It is easier to grow less slug friendly plants.

There are consequences to the use of chemicals to control slugs. Slug pellets contain meteldehyde and a dead slug, fed to a bird such as a Song Thrush equates to a poisoned, dead Song Thrush. Remember the statistics about bird populations in Chapter 1? Farmers use metaldehyde to control slugs in crops. And when there is a wet British Summer or after a dry Summer such as 1976 or 2018 the residue washes off the fields **and gets into our water supply.**

Lets take the River Stour in 2013 where metaldehyde was measured at 100 times the EU acceptable limit and said to be of "no danger" by our local authorities within the local water supply. (as reported, again, in the Guardian) How many years would it take for any consequences to be felt? What do we really know to be "safe"?? In fact, reservoirs were found to contain metaldehyde in 81 of 647 water sources though said to be at low levels. However does anybody really know what a "safe level" is, in the context of a possible lifetime drinking this water? After all, it doesn't do much good to a slug, does it? In August 2019 the Times newspaper investigated rivers in the UK and found that dangerous pollutants had reached the highest levels ever in the modern era. 86% failed to meet EU standards.

metaldehyde is just one of these pollutants and it was being phased out by 2020, but this decision, as I go to press, has been reversed. Why do we continue to allow this to happen?

Anyway back to the point of this section. In the appendix and throughout this book, plants that are prone to slug attack are mentioned, not so that you don't want to buy them, but so you are aware the plant could need much more attention! And whatever you do, do not go anywhere near slug pellets or anything that has chemicals within it. And this leads me nicely into...

RULE 4—NO PESTICIDES AND NO WEEDKILLER

The first one is a no brainer if you want to support wildlife. Fly spray in a house is poison. If it kills another creature, how good is it for you? Just let the wasp or fly out of the house. Open the door! There has to be a balance in the world and that is provided by all creatures. Leave real pest infestations to professionals.

In our gardens, in MOST circumstances we should not be interfering with the natural balance of plants, except where mankind has allowed an alien invasive species to threaten the natives such as Japanese Knotweed (Victorians fault, that one, they awarded it a medal for being pretty... it is now illegal to plant it)

See chapter 11 where I explain how I do garden without harming any creatures, and seldom, if ever, do I use weedkiller.

The problem with chemical weedkiller is that it kills insects, not just plants. There are "insect friendly" options which work, but check what ingredients are in them, and whether the insect friendly claims are actually true. A soap based solution seems to me to be much better than chemicals, at the time of writing.

*Above: The purple **Alcea or Hollyhock** is a very good bee plant. The tall spires of Verbascum are of lesser interest to bees but are used by moth caterpillars .The Yellow Cornflower **Centaurea macrocephala** is good for bees and hoverflies but flowers briefly. The Evening Primrose **Oenothera** (front left) is good for moths and can flower for months. These plants have different facets which produce different "scores" from my research and will attract and sustain different insect populations.*

Many (not all) weeds are just wild flowers that can be happy in your garden and in some circumstances are really good for insects. But be careful what you buy from a garden centre as...

An additional (and serious) problem is that some garden centres sell plants that are dripping with insecticide!

Ask your garden centre whether this is the case.

Don't buy plants that could poison your local insects whilst ironically promising to be "insect friendly" on the plant label!

Don't support a garden centre that kills or poisons insects by using chemicals on the plants they supply!

A study from University of Sussex's Professor Dave Goulson did find 'bee-friendly' plants for sale with traces of one of the three neonicotinoid-based insecticide products banned by the EU(imidacloprid, thiamethoxam or clothianidin).There are mail order plant suppliers such as Rosybee.com who use no pesticides on their plants.

RULE 5—NO INVASIVE OR "MONSTER" PLANTS

Some plants are too large for a small garden, or invasive. Some may make poor use of the space they occupy for insects. A Scottish Thistle may have glorious flowers for bees but will be 3 metres high and almost as wide. The percentage of the plant that is a flower is very small. So a good plant for using space would be a foxglove. It has spires of flowers that lead vertically upwards, but does not take up much room on the ground and has a long flowering period.

"Monster" plants is just my term for those that are just not helpful additions in most gardens which means that they have any of the following characteristics

- to contain poisonous sap (Euphorbia species for example) or If they could cause an allergic response on exposure to skin. Rue and Aconitum are examples of this and plants like that should be avoided.

- Those that are very fast spreading in a garden (invasive) or produce copious seed and self seed everywhere.

There are varying degrees of hazard from plants, I'm not saying you cannot plant a Euphorbia. But it has milky sap that will make you blind if it gets in your eyes. Many people have had allergic skin reactions. It is however my personal choice that I avoid this type of plant.

Always look at garden centre labels, for information as to potential hazards.

RULE 6 - USE SUCCESSION PLANTING

Concentrated Ecology Planting is a type of succession planting, but only using plants that are very beneficial to insects.

Basically, if a plant blooms in May, and then does nothing for the rest of the year, or dies back, then allow a plant that blooms in July or later to take over some or all of that spot. This makes the area *twice as productive* for insects such as bees. The first plant can be left there, many will tolerate being shaded out until next early Spring.

Planting plans incorporating this idea can be found in Chapter 12.

RULE 7 OBSERVATION

This is fun! If you are at a Garden Centre, looking for a certain plant from my list (often I will specify a particular variety such as Heuchera "Coral Bells") do see if there are bees visiting one plant rather than another. Check that they are actually feeding from the flowers consistently.

This is a way of validating insect research, but will help you see the differences between how good certain plants are in comparison to others. I think it will surprise you how big the differences are. I have told you my truth, it is fun to discover your own…

HOW TO USE THIS BOOK

This book is designed to be easy to read and to understand whilst providing a lot of information. To help this you need to note the following.

Latin Names—Plants are identified using the **Latin Names** (as still used by Garden Centres) and shown in **Bold** though I have also used **common names** where possible. Most plants are easy to obtain, I have stated where they are not!

Glossary—There are different terms used in gardening and in the description of insects, see the glossary for explanation of what they are.

Score for Pollinating Insects— The results were achieved using **a method explained in chapter 3** and principles shown there. You will need to read that chapter to understand the scores.

A selection of the best plants that are easy to grow are shown in Chapters 4, 5, 6, 10 and 12.

Plant Sizes where not otherwise stated are Very Small—below 15 cms. Small below 1 metre Medium—below 1.5 metres and Large above 1.5 metres in height.

The **Appendix** shows all the results (good and bad!) and gives you the opportunity to "audit" what is in your garden.

You can add up the scores for plants currently in your garden, to replace or change plants that score little for those that have a high score for insects.

Following the plans or rules in this book will make your garden a valuable place for insects!

Bombus pascuorum, the Common Carder Bee, on **Helianthus "Lemon Queen"** on October 2nd.

CHAPTER 3 -
HOW THE BEST PLANTS WERE CHOSEN

Above, Small Tortoiseshell Butterfly on Sneezeweed, Helenium, 17th July.

The monitoring sites were gardens around 120 metres above sea level in the South of England. Climate variation is great here. Spring can arrive plus or minus two weeks, so flowering periods are average figures or the most likely to occur. I have visited many other gardens to supplement this knowledge. Even if dates may change from year to year this information is invaluable in planning a succession of plants that bloom to help insects, so that forage is consistent. The gardens were prone to frost, on clay and chalk in the North Downs of Surrey.

The best plants for insects are listed starting in Chapter 4 but for now, here is my explanation of how I got to that result.

The process of looking at insects had the following aspects

1) **Recording** of information

2) **Interpretation** of the information to produce **results**

3) **Other factors** to decide which plants were to be recommended

Recording of information was by observation of the habits of bees, butterflies and other insects which I started in 1993 but in a greater way from 1997.

To validate the research I spent much of 2017—2019 looking at many gardens and situations of wildlife plants. I did this mainly in Southern England. I also visited botanical gardens as far apart as Dublin and Northern Italy.

Bees rely partly on the direction of the Suns' rays to find previously discovered food sources but can navigate on cloudy days.   Most insects will need to stay out of the way on very rainy or windy days. Small insects retreat into shade on hot days as exposure to the mid-day sun is damaging.

So I defined an **Optimum time** for the study of all insects as **a still, sunny or bright day between 9 o'clock and 5 o'clock when the temperature is 15 degrees Celsius but less than 25 degrees Celsius.**

The temperature would often be well below 15 degrees Celcius from January to April, or October to December so results could not have an optimum time measurement in that period. Also my initial results in previous years were based upon much greater populations. There has been a huge decline in all insects in recent years. So I had to adjust the way these earlier results were interpreted to deal with potential inconsistency or visit other locations with a greater number of insects.

I drew a comparison (ratio) between plants that were flowering at the same time and the broad number of insects that were about. If there were few insects but they all visited one plant, this was a positive result for that plant. If there were many insects about and a high number feeding on that same plant, that confirms that plant is good. But other plants visited would also score but, in a comparative sense a judgement can be made if they are not as attractive as a food source when sufficient populations are about. This comparison is in fact insect **preference.**

Preference - In the same way as we have a favourite food we like to eat, bees in particular, have favourite flowers that they will visit, above others that are blooming at the same time. However they will go back to other flowers, if the preference plant is not about.

An example is Teucrium versus Lavender. Bees love Lavender, but often prefer Teucrium if it is available so scoring has to reflect this.

Flowering plants also need to be growing well to be flowering in the first place. I discarded results from small plants or flowers that were not fully out.

In recording the results I felt it would be too confusing for me (and others) to allocate scores for too many types of insects.   I divided the insect population into four groups, weighted the results towards Bees and then Butterflies by allowing them a maximum score of four symbols each (40 points). In this book I also mention particular insects of note for individual plants with a particular focus on those you are likely to find in your garden such as common types of bumblebee and also solitary bees. (See Chapter 8 for more information about this) The symbol ❤ denotes this in the plant chapters.

For Hoverflies and Other Insects (Flies etc)   I allowed a maximum of three symbols (30 points) This makes a maximum possible total of 140 points for all these elements, though no plant actually scored this amount.

Just some of the 700 plants that I have personally grown or studied for this book

The flowering period of plants was then added to the score weighted towards those that bloom more than 21 days. Those plants that flower less, whilst worthy, are making less of a contribution with the space that they occupy over time.

Much less energy is expended by an insect flying to a known food source. Imagine if you drove to Clacket Lane service station on the M25 for a coffee, lunch and petrol... and it was shut! You have expended all that fuel for nothing to get there, and maybe you are now hungry, with a near empty fuel tank that cannot get you home. This is the only study that rewards long flowering plants, with **a score of 1 extra point for every 4 days over a 21 day flowering period.**

The resulting total provides, I feel, an accurate, relative assessment of how attractive the type of plant was in my study. It represents thousands of hours spent looking at both plants and insects. I also validated my research against verified information just to make sure I had not missed out on anything.

This does not mean that a study completed where you live will have the same results but there is no doubt in my mind that selecting plants that I have picked for this book will make your garden a haven for insect wildlife. Removing plants that score lower than 30 and replacing them with pollinator favoured alternatives will improve the garden you already have. Even planting a hanging basket with insect friendly plants makes a difference if you don't have a garden. Every contribution will help.

The point is that the insects have said what they like here, not me! The difference between a plant that makes little impact to insects and one that does is comparable to the score, making it possible to make your garden so good for them, that you really can help **save our Insects!**

These keys are referred to in Chapter 4,5,6,7 10,12 and Appendix

KEY FOR BEES

>>>> *Bees constantly visit the plant which is rarely left unattended during optimum time conditions and sufficient populations. Top scoring plant in my research also taking into consideration preference over other plants.*

>>> *Bees visit the plant with definite and consistent interest during more than 50% of the optimum time with sufficient populations,*

>> *Bees visit the plant and obtain some benefit but on an irregular, sporadic basis.*

> *Bees rarely visit this plant.*

KEY FOR BUTTERFLIES (INCLUDING MOTHS WHERE STATED)

Butterflies rarely seen off this plant during optimum times and sufficient populations. The top plants in my research.

Butterflies seen feeding on this plant during optimum times.

or # *Butterflies have some/little interest in this plant*

Also see Chapter 9 for information about Moths relating to this study

KEY FOR HOVERFLIES

*** *Hoverflies favourite plants. Often seen visiting and feeding (and hovering) where there are sufficient populations. The top plants in my study.*

** *Hoverflies do visit and feed on this plant less than 50% of the optimum time where there are sufficient populations*

* *Hoverflies visit this plant on a sporadic infrequent basis*

KEY FOR OTHER INSECTS - FLIES (including very small flies) WASPS and others where specifically stated.

~~~ *A plant often seen visited by flies and other insects. The top plants in my research*

~~ *A plant where other insects are found on a regular basis*

~ *A small but noticeable component is the visiting of other insects*

❤ (within the chapters only) denotes an individual insect which has a particular liking for this plant

CHAPTER 4 - THE BEST PLANTS MARCH TO JUNE

CROCUS - LATIN NAMES CROCUS VERNUS (DUTCH CROCUS)

CROCUS CHRYSANTHUS, CROCUS FLAVUS, CROCUS TOMMASINIANUS

TYPICAL FLOWERING PERIOD 25/02—31/03 (PICTURED ABOVE 11/3)

SYMBOLS >>>* POINTS SCORED 49 VERY SMALL PERENNIAL BULB

When Queen bumblebees finally take to flight after hibernation this is the plant they head for first, no contest. This plant provides pollen and nectar for them at a crucial time. The Yellow Crocus (Crocus flavus) is visited less, in my experience, than purple and white varieties. Easily obtained as bags of bulbs (buy 100 to get a decent show) usually described as "mixed crocus" the plants are sensitive to temperature and will bloom earlier in gardens which are more protected from the cold. There are few other insects about in March, but early hoverflies will also visit. Tulips and Daffodils are very poor for insects, so go for the Crocus!

TOP TIP

To get the longest flowering period buy as many different varieties of Spring crocus as possible. They are often available as mixed bulbs. Also plant new bulbs every year as the bulbs already in the ground will bloom later.

Taking this advice you should have a month of pleasure from these beautiful flowers though note the flowering period can start in early February.

PLANTING ADVICE

Plant in the lawn about 8 centimetres deep. Put grit sand or gravel beneath them to stop the bulbs from rotting in Winter wet soils. Squirrels love eating or disrupting these bulbs. Put some wire netting above the bulbs to prevent losses when the ground is not frozen. You can cut the grass during April when the leaves (which follow the flowers) have died back. They like an open position and do best for the bees where they catch the Winter sunshine after mid-day.

HEATHER (IRISH HEATH)   LATIN NAMES   (SEE BELOW)

TYPICAL FLOWERING PERIOD 20/1—25/4   (PICTURED ABOVE 27/2)

SYMBOLS >>>>~ POINTS SCORED 94 SMALL SHRUB (70 x 40CM MAX)**

A plant that flowers from the depths of Winter well beyond the early breath of Spring. This is a fantastic plant for any bees emerging from hibernation. I have found that almost all plants are good for bees with some white flowered varieties the best. On 8th February I watched many honeybees feeding on white and pink heather on a still day at just 9 Celsius at a local garden centre. At such a temperature, they were not far from the hives. It was a pleasurable experience knowing they were gathering much needed supplies, making the most of a brief opportunity. For me it was the perfect time to select proven individual plants. At home, on my hill, honey bees were not about at all. But I know, having planted these plants that attracted so many bees at the garden centre that when the temperature does rise enough, they will be along to join the Bumblebees already feeding. Also see Chapter 12, Heather Garden.

Recommended varieties (tolerant of lime) and easily obtained with Latin Names (often described as Spring Flowering Heather in garden centres) are

Erica x darleyensis "White Perfection", "Ghost Hills" (Pink) "Golden Perfect" (White)

Erica carnea "Diana Young", "Rosalie" and "Challenger" (Dark pink) Erica erigena "WT Rackliff" (White)

PLANTING ADVICE

Erica have varieties that are tolerant of some chalk or lime (alkaline soil) and others that will not grow other than in acid soil. It is a good idea to plant slightly raised above the existing ground with Ericaceous compost, anyway, as in that way the plant will get used to any alkalinity gradually. September flowering Heather is a great bee plant under the Latin name **Calluna** or Ling. Most of these only grow well in Acid Soil and are mentioned in the appendix.

Pictured above - **Common Carder Bee** *Bombus pascuorum* on Pulmonaria "Opal"

LUNGWORT – LATIN NAME PULMONARIA

TYPICAL FLOWERING PERIOD 20/02 – 25/04

SYMBOLS >>>>*~ POINTS SCORED 76 VERY SMALL PERENNIAL

♥ HAIRY FOOTED FLOWER BEE—ANTHOPHORA PLUMIPES

This is a very important early bee plant. Time and again other candidates at this time of the year were ignored, and the time spent on this plant dwarfed all others except Heather. And like heather, it is worth putting aside some space for a good clump of this plant. It is tolerant of shade and also is happy for other plants to grow over it during the year. The best of many varieties of Pulmonaria are...

Pulmonaria "Trevi Fountain" (Blue with Mauve emerging flowers—this is one of the best and longest flowering varieties on which the flowering period above is based)

Pulmonaria "Opal" (Pearl Blue or Creamy)

Pulmonaria "Dark Vader"   (Rose Mauve. Star Wars fans should buy this one!)

Pulmonaria "Blue Ensign" (Royal Blue)   **"Redstart"** (Red)

Pulmonaria "Raspberry Splash" Was still attractive to bees, but not as frequently as other varieties, possibly because of the smaller flowers.

TOP TIP

Pulmonaria can look tatty come August. Cut off the leaves after flowering, water well, and a new burst of leaves (sometimes mottled white in some varieties) will come through and look good until Autumn. These plants will self seed and are easily divided, just water them well and they will establish quickly.

PUSSY WILLOW LATIN NAME SALIX CAPREA "KILMARNOCK"

TYPICAL FLOWERING PERIOD 01/03— 25/03

SYMBOLS >>>*~ POINTS SCORED 50 WEEPING TREE (1.5 METRES)

Garden Centres often have rows of this small weeping tree all of them all producing the "pussy willow" blooms. Do buy a plant that is being visited by an insect or three and one that has many more buds to come to show that the plant is a good one. Other types of willow are too "wild" for a small garden. Being a type of willow, it must not dry out. That is the most common reason for plants to be lost.

TOP TIP

This is great planted in a large pot with Aconites, Crocus, Anemone and Snowdrops around the base. The willow will offer little however for the rest of the year it is otherwise a dull plant. My suggestion is to plant some poached egg plant seeds (Limnanthes) to provide interest in June, they will then self seed, to provide a green base through which the bulbs will bloom again next year.

PERENNIAL WALLFLOWER ERYSIMUM "BOWLES MAUVE"

TYPICAL FLOWERING PERIOD 20/03— 20/08

SYMBOLS >>>### POINTS SCORED 117 SMALL SHRUB**

♥ PAINTED LADY BUTTERFLY —*VANESSA CARDUI*

Erysimum "Bowles Mauve" above left with "Fragrant Sunshine" right

A flowering period over 160 days for "Bowles Mauve" the best of the Erysimums makes this a remarkable plant for any garden. Though often in the last month or so the flowers are dwindling. The plant is very attractive to emerging bees early in the season, and visited by bee flies, butterflies and hoverflies later on.

This is a good all rounder plant for insects, though bee interest tails off a little as they explore other (presumably more exciting) forage options in the main season.

"Bowles Mauve" is a long established reliable and easily obtained plant and no other variety comes close in terms of flowering period and ease of cultivation.

Other perennial plants are available under the description Erysimum such as orange, yellow and mixtures. The main enemy of these is Winter wet causing root rot.

There is also a traditional "wallflower" biennial, and you can buy this type from garden centres in late Winter often with bare roots and in many bright colours. They score a little for early bees but are not nearly as good as **"Bowles Mauve"**

TOP TIP Take cuttings of this plant, it may not last for more than 3 years, unless deeply rooted within a wall, the clue is in the name!! Trim it to a rounded shape if it looks like it has almost stopped flowering and it will look good for the next year.

PINCUSHION FLOWER —LATIN NAME ASTRANTIA MAJOR

TYPICAL FLOWERING PERIOD   06/06—06/07 SYMBOLS >>>*~#

POINTS SCORED 68 SMALL PERENNIAL

♥ HONEY BEE *APIS MELLIFERA*

Astrantia is another plant slugs love to eat but grown on the edge of a path and in big clumps it is a brilliant bee plant in June. The white variety **"Alba"** and near white **"Shaggy"** is in favour here as more vigorous than some of the more bred (and beautiful) varieties.

They are all very attractive to honey bees. Give this good soil, and keep it watered every day until it is established. However if you are like me, the dusky red varieties such as **"Venice"** and **"Roma"** will probably tempt you. But they will also tempt the slugs. A mulch or covering of gravel around the plants will be helpful here.

ROCK ROSE—LATIN NAME CISTUS CORBARIENSIS

TYPICAL FLOWERING PERIOD 15/05-17/06 (PICTURED 31/05)

SYMBOLS >>>>##* POINTS SCORED 99 MEDIUM EVERGREEN SHRUB**

The genus Cistus or sun rose / rock rose, have plants of varying hardiness and large flowers from white, to white blotched to dark pink. The plant pictured above, **Cistus corbariensis** is the best. A vigorous plant in a sunny position will obtain 1.5 metres in height and width.   It flowers profusely for one month. As it produces many flowers (each one only lasts a couple of days at most) the amount of sustenance available for insects is generous. Hoverflies find it easy to feed on the plants.   It is possible to cut it back a little after flowering.   It is also easy to take a non flowering shoot and increase by cuttings.   Cistus plants are sun worshippers, so don't put it in shade and think it will actually grow for you. It does not need a sun hat, even if you do! Avoid the related **" Thrive"** which is not favoured by bees in the same way.

OTHER VARIETIES - **Cistus purpureus** is a large shrub up to 2 metres with flowers from July to September of pink with five red central blotches. Hardy in my garden for 10 years so far. **Cistus pulverulentus** medium sized but pink flowers without the blotches. **Cistus "Snow Fire"** has white flowers with red blotches, I have found this to be a good container plant, but it may not always get through the Winter.

All of these are worth their place for insects, but do not flower as profusely as **Cistus corbariensis** (which is the best option).

WELSH POPPY —LATIN NAME MECONOPSIS CAMBRICA

TYPICAL FLOWERING PERIOD 24/04-20/08 (PICTURED 27/05)

SYMBOLS >>>>~ POINTS SCORED 100 SMALL PERENNIAL**

❤ BOMBUS LUCORUM - WHITE TAILED BUMBLEBEE

A charming plant which is a native wild flower.   Bees love the yellow, sometimes orange flowers. Unlike other poppies that have a "splash and dash" flowering period of a few weeks this does flower from Mid May for a month...and then when it wants to at any other time of the year.   It is useful in a shady position though does need some sun each day to do well and has a liking for self seeding in cracks in pavements, walls and "in between" areas.

TOP TIP Having several Welsh Poppy plants and trying them in different positions will mean you will have flowers at different times of the year. Seed is easy to collect and germinate, cut off the seedpods to promote more flowers. Never move once planted as the taproot is sensitive to such things. Many years ago, my mum took a small poppy plant home from a garden in Devon, resting it on a wet piece of tissue paper during the 7 hour journey. A legion of other flowers eventually came, in the garden of my childhood from this one plant.

AVENS —LATIN NAME GEUM TYPICAL FLOWERING PERIOD 15/05-15/06

SYMBOLS >>** POINTS SCORED 48 SMALL PERENNIAL

Geums are popular in garden centres and can be found as **"Totally Tangerine" "Mrs J Bradshaw" (Red), "Lady Stratheden" (Yellow) and "Mango Lassie"** They have a flowering period around 4 weeks and like moisture retentive soil. Drying out will lead to a sulky plant that may not return. The response of bees to Geum was sporadic within my results. Some days favoured, some days abandoned. I suggest you observe, in May, at the garden centre to decide on a purchase, or not. I think this is a lower preference plant but bees will still visit it.

LADIES SMOCK —LATIN NAME HESPERIS MATRONALIS

TYPICAL FLOWERING PERIOD 20/04-20/06

SYMBOLS >>####** POINTS SCORED 95 MEDIUM BIENNIAL

This has gentle purple or white flowers which are attractive to moths and butterflies including the ♥ Orange Tip Butterfly Anthocharis cardamines found commonly in gardens. This butterfly may use this as a secondary food plant but survival of caterpillars to maturity is said to be poor. Garlic mustard (Alliaria petiolata) is a wild flower often found in gardens, and a first preference plant. But what do you do if you find butterfly eggs on either of these?

Check to see there are eggs on the stems or leaves (small, apricot coloured ovals) If so, avoid cutting back the plant as the caterpillars will eat the seed pods. Cover with very fine mesh, making a tent above the plant with canes to support, this will prevent predation until the chrysalis stage.

Otherwise, you can cut Hesperis back after flowering. It will then flower again for the benefit of butterflies.

Above **Scabious "Butterfly Blue"** living up to its name visited by a **Meadow Brown**

SCABIOUS (AND PLANTS REFERRED TO AS "SCABIOUS")

♥ MEADOW BROWN BUTTERFLY - MANIOLA JURTINA

This is a very large family of plants from small to gigantic, described as "Scabious" and almost universally very good for pollinating insects. Also having told you to avoid anything that looks like a "double" flower, well they look like they are, but the flower structure is perfect for insects.

PINCUSHION FLOWER—LATIN NAME SCABIOSA COLUMBARIA

TYPICAL FLOWERING PERIOD 15/05– 01/08

SYMBOLS >>>###* POINTS SCORED 90 SMALL PERENNIAL

A very common variety is **Scabiosa columbaria 'Butterfly Blue'** which is a small perennial that will flower from late Spring to Autumn if you keep deadheading the plant, it is brilliant for butterflies bees and hoverflies. There are pink varieties of this too but this is the strongest / best variety to grow.

GIANT SCABIOUS—LATIN NAME—CEPHALARIA GIGANTEA

TYPICAL FLOWERING PERIOD 20/06— 01/08

SYMBOLS >>>>###***~ POINTS SCORED 121 GIANT PERENNIAL

A large plant though it does not spread aggressively. With me, I tried to get away with a semi shaded position at the back of a border. It showed its disapproval flopping and flouncing its tall, wiry, flower stems onto nearby plants from a great height. It needs support, in other words and at least a few hours of sunshine each day.

KNAUTIA MACEDONICA (MACEDONIAN SCABIOUS) POINTS SCORED 125 SYMBOLS >>>>####*** TYPICAL FLOWERING PERIOD 25/5 - 27/7

KNAUTIA ARVENSIS (FIELD SCABIOUS—UK NATIVE) TYPICAL FLOWERING PERIOD 20/6 - 20/7   POINTS SCORED 109 >>>####***

Knautia arvensis is the flower of meadows and fields with lilac blue flowers attractive to most insects. A native wild flower which is also the food plant of the **Marsh Fritillary, Bee Hawk Moth** and a micro moth known as the **Brassy Long-horn.**

Knautia macedonica is available in pink, red, and lilac In garden centres often described as **"Melton Pastels". "Red Knight"** and **"Thunder and Lightning"** are also available. The standard red plant (closest to the original wild flower) is the best one and liked very much by honey bees, all bumblebees, solitary bees and butterflies It flops over other plants much like its larger cousin **Cephalaria** and can be plagued by mildew. It is best planted in a sunny, open position where it is relatively tolerant of conditions.

Cut back and keep both these flowers watered after flowering as it will then flower again. Both are candidates for meadow plantings and are small perennial plants.

COMFREY— LATIN NAMES SYMPHYTUM OFFICINALE /UPLANDICUM /IBERICUM   TYPICAL

FLOWERING PERIOD 15/04— 10/06

SYMBOLS >>>* POINTS SCORED   54 SMALL PERENNIAL GROUND COVER

The native comfrey **(Symphytum officinale)** grows over 1 metre, blooming in June and July. Invasiveness is the potential problem with this comfrey in a garden.

Most of the plants you find at garden centres will be small ground cover types of **Symphytum uplandicum** or **ibericum.** These are early blooming plants, offering early rewards for insects at a time when there are not many about.

In many respects I prefer **Pulmonaria** which blooms at a similar time and is also shade tolerant. Comfrey scores though in its tolerance of much deeper, even dry shade and growing under trees. It is a great plant for an "awkward spot" and the experts out there in management of forage sites definitely prefer to plant this.

These ground cover plants are available in white pink or washed out blue but all colours are much visited by honeybees, bumblebees and solitary bees.

It has an additional use as removed leaves can be used to speed up the progress of compost decomposition on a compost heap. Rotting leaves in a bucket make a stinky, high potash fertiliser after 14 days which, after dilution, can be watered around plants.

OTHER EARLY FLOWERING PLANTS

WINDFLOWER LATIN NAME ANEMONE BLANDA

TYPICAL FLOWERING PERIOD 25/03 - 20/04 SCORE >>> 37 POINTS

This small plant has blue or white flowers and is most attractive to early bumblebees. This is happy in a woodland and shady situation but does not like to dry out.

WALL CRESS LATIN NAME—ARABIS

TYPICAL FLOWERING PERIOD

SYMBOLS >>* SCORE 36 20/04 - 15/05

A useful rock garden plant that takes up little room and offers early rewards to insects. **Arabis "Grandiflora Rosea"** is recommended. Avoid variegated varieties that flower less. This does not get floored by slugs, unlike Aubretia.

COWSLIP- LATIN NAME - PRIMULA VERIS

TYPICAL FLOWERING PERIOD 31/03— 05/05

SYMBOLS >>># POINTS SCORED 49 VERY SMALL PERENNIAL

Cowslips are native plants to the UK that flower early and are much visited by emerging bees. They like moist soil and grow well in corners of a lawn however they do need damp soil and are unlikely to prosper in a dry area. Wild flower food plant of the **Duke of Burgundy Fritillary Butterfly, Plain Clay** and **Northern Rustic Moths.**

Primrose (Primula vulgaris) which blooms at the same time did not atract many insects in my research but in less cold gardens than my own is pollinated by bees including solitary bees. Later primulas such as the "candelabra" type found in Garden Centres are beautiful flowers but limited in terms of attracting insects.

BISTORT - LATIN NAME PERSICARIA BISTORTA

TYPICAL FLOWERING PERIOD 25/04— 20/05

SYMBOLS >>>#~~ POINTS SCORED 66 SMALL PERENNIAL

The genus **Persicaria** (which used to be Polygonum) offers a variety of plants some of which have no value to wildlife at all. However the common **Bistort,** a UK native flower, is a good plant despite its habit of creeping about in the garden (it is easy to remove plants that go a little too far)

As an early plant for bees (and early interested flies) this is good. Early butterflies will also visit the plant. After flowering it tends to vanish, meaning other plants can take its space. The flowers are light pink and pleasant enough in any garden scheme.

FALSE ROCK CRESS/ AUBRETIA   LATIN NAME AUBRETA

TYPICAL FLOWERING PERIOD 01/03 - 30/04

SYMBOLS >>~~ SCORE 55 POINTS

The small flowers of Aubretia are available in purples red and dark pinks however it is the standard mid purple variety, **Aubrieta hybrida "Hendersonii"** which is most vigorous and better against slugs. This is attractive to bees purely as it is an early plant, when better alternatives become available it is visited less by bees.

Allium "Mount Everest" at Great Dixter Garden, East Sussex

THE ONION FAMILY —LATIN NAME ALLIUM

The Onion family are very important to pollinators (very much a top tier plant for bees) and fundamental to the concept of Ecology Gardening as they are bulbs.

Bulbs have their own energy store, which takes up little space, meaning that they can grow and "peek" in between (or even through) other plants without consequence to their own growth. They increase the forage productivity of a small area.

Alliums struggle to flower more than 20 days on the whole, however they are a very important additional ingredient for the insect garden, with most scoring strongly.

ALLIUM "PURPLE SENSATION"

TYPICAL FLOWERING PERIOD 07/05— 25/05

SYMBOLS   >>>>## POINTS SCORED 90 PERENNIAL BULB**

The pick of the crop, so to speak this and has flowers that are very attractive to a wide range of insects. Pictured above right and left (Purple)

ALLIUM "GLOBEMASTER"

Similar to above but lighter colour (pictured centre above)

ALLIUM "MOUNT EVEREST" (also "MOUNT BLANC) (Picture previous page)

Not as long flowered as the purple variety but almost as attractive to bees

ALLIUM CRISTOPHII TYPICAL FLOWERING PERIOD 20/5—10/6

Flowers later than the above plants with huge exploding flower heads. Total score is 60 points

ALLIUM ATROPURPUREUM has small dark rose coloured flat flower heads and will be in flower later than the above alliums in mid June.

ALLIUM SPHAEROCEPHALON

TYPICAL FLOWERING PERIOD 07/07— 27/07

SYMBOLS >>>>##* POINTS SCORED 90 PERENNIAL BULB**

It has no real leaves and after flowering and cutting back you would not know it was there. Despite a flowering period of 18 days or so, this is a very useful plant to pop in between others.   But as with all alliums, I do wish it would flower for longer!

CHIVES—ALLIUM SCHOENOPRASUM 02/06— 21/06

♥ RED TAILED BUMBLEBEE *BOMBUS LAPIDARIUS*

Chives is a herb and is also very attractive to bumblebees and honey bees.

TOP TIP Buy these plants in bulb form, it is so much cheaper than buying a garden centre grown plant! Also consider buying a lot of these, and mix and match them for the longest flowering period. They can be planted right next to other plants and will disappear from view by the time Summer perennials have got going.

They are often available in "mixed" bags of **"Nigrum", "Purple Sensation", and "Mount Everest "**which are related and flower at the same time. Put some gravel beneath them when planting, they do not want to rot in Winter cold and wet!

PLUME THISTLE - CIRSIUM RIVULARE

SYMBOLS >>> SCORE 60 Points**

Very much beloved at the Chelsea flower show of recent years, **Cirsium rivulare "Atropurpureum"** has dark red flowers rich in pollen and nectar that flower in Spring. Pictured above on 15th May. There is also **"Trevors Blue Wonder"** (Trevor needs to go to the opticians as the plant is NOT blue) Even gardening gurus say it can be a bit difficult to grow. It likes moist, well drained, rich soil.

I prefer **Cirsium tuberosum** (Scores 76 Points) which is available from Great Dixter Nursery and others on the net. This medium perennial flowers June to August.

All thistles are attractive to insects but many are pernicious weeds. **"Tuberosum"** is originally a very rare UK Native plant. The foliage of these plants is most weed like, as with all thistles, but the lovely flowers put it a cut above a dandelion.

FOXGLOVES - LATIN NAME DIGITALIS PURPUREA (NATIVE)

TYPICAL FLOWERING PERIOD 19/05—05/07

SYMBOLS >>>>* POINTS SCORED 62 LARGE PERENNIAL

♥ GARDEN BUMBLEBEE *BOMBUS HORTORUM*

One of my favourite wildlife plants. They give so much with their spires of flowers, don't take up much space and happily grow in light shade in ordinary soil.

Pretty much all types are very attractive to bumblebees so it comes down to which would grow best for you and how much they cost.

There is a dizzying variety of plants available. I find I do have to replant some every year despite claims of certain plants being "Perennial"

Digitalis purpurea " Excelsior Hybrids" Various colours, the native plant on steroids, up to 2 metres tall, very beautiful and pictured above.

Digitalis purpurea "Alba" - White and close to the native white flower.

Digitalis purpurea " Suttons Apricot" Apricot-ish flowers

Digitalis purpurea "Pams Choice" My choice too. White/darker maroon blotches

Digitalis lutea - delicate pale yellow variety. **Digitalis parviflora**—smaller flowers and unusual burnt orange colours **Digitalis mertonensis.** Dark dusky pink blooms.

Avoid Digitalis lanata, the woolly foxglove due to concerns over possible poisoning or intoxicating of solitary bees. Avoid expensive cherry red plants that look like Penstemons. Buy one of those instead.

Also see the design chapter (12) for planting advice on Foxgloves

RED HOT POKER - LATIN NAME KNIPHOFIA CAULESCENS

TYPICAL FLOWERING PERIOD 25/05—15/06

SYMBOLS >>>>* POINTS SCORED 57 MEDIUM PERENNIAL

Kniphofia as a genus contains a large number of "poker" plants which produce dramatic rockets of bloom that last a few weeks at most. They used to be regarded as not fully hardy. I took the plant above from a previous garden, to my current one. It has been in my front garden for years, and it has survived frosts of –10 celsius.

Other varieties can be tricky. Often they flower late in the season. Kniphofia needs full sun, and isn't one to allow other plants to shade over it. This plant needs space. Slugs and snails eat the flowers and only obsessively picking them off the spikes will save them. If you are really treated, you might see a blue tit visit the plant to drink the nectar which is in plentiful supply from this South African native plant. It is also worth trying **Kniphofia rooperii** (flowers September to October with orange flowers) and "**Bees Lemon"** (September, yellow).

BUGLE PLANT - LATIN NAME AJUGA REPTANS

TYPICAL FLOWERING PERIOD 03/05—03/06

**SYMBOLS >>*~~ POINTS SCORED 58
VERY SMALL PERENNIAL**

Though attention of insects is sporadic, this has been good for small flies who appear to hide within the leaves and for bees such as solitary bees. It is happy being shaded out by other perennials later in the season. Not a top tier wildlife plant but useful due to its tolerance.

Always buy this in bloom and look for insect interest, dark red leaved varieties are mostly good, though the UK native, green leaved bugle plant is the best of the bunch. Avoid buying plants NOT in flower, as some are foliage plants, not flower plants.

NINEBARK - LATIN NAME PHYSOCARPUS

TYPICAL FLOWERING PERIOD 20/05—15/06

SYMBOLS >>>~ MAX POINTS SCORED 57 LARGE SHRUB**

I can see learned gardeners turning up their noses at the inclusion of this plant. Put simply, its far from a favourite among experts. But, for a few brief weeks, a mature plant attracts bees and hoverflies in great numbers, before returning back to its previous state thereafter. Pictured above is **Physocarpus "Diablo".**

TOP TIP

"Diablo" is sometimes looked down upon, but new better varieties are being bred which may retain the appeal for bees, such as **"Lady in Red"** Also **"Darts Gold"** is a (dubious) light yellow green leaved variety. Avoid Chalk soil.

ROSE - LATIN NAME - ROSA TYPICAL FLOWERING PERIOD 30/05—30/7

The vast majority of the hundreds of varieties of roses are of little use to insects. The extra petals of double flowers just prevent pollinators getting a reward, or a sufficient reward is not there. So I start off, on behalf of insects, not being a fan. The exceptions are single flowered roses which are closest to natural species and the monster triffid that is **Rosa rugosa.** However Roses provide only pollen, and not nectar. So I think there are better choices for the Summer garden though the insect above is not in agreement.   Roses such as **Rosa gallica "Officianalis"** in the picture are very old varieties and partial exceptions to the rule.

WEIGELA - LATIN NAME WEIGELA

TYPICAL FLOWERING PERIOD 20/05—01/07

SYMBOLS >>>*~ MAX POINTS SCORED 61 MEDIUM SIZED SHRUB

"Bristol Ruby" is an old variety with penstemon like flowers, is best for bumblebees. The shocking variegated pink and yellow green options are best avoided.

SOLOMONS SEAL - LATIN NAME - POLYGONATUM (NATIVE)

TYPICAL FLOWERING PERIOD 01/05—20/05

SYMBOLS >>~~ MAX POINTS SCORED 40 SMALL PERENNIAL

💙 SOLOMONS SEAL SAWFLY PHYMATOCERA ATERRIMA

The Solomons Seal sawfly will often eat all the leaves of this but it is tough enough to cope with it. Otherwise, the flowers are attractive to bees. The only drawback is the brief time in flower. However this is very shade tolerant, growing where other plants would most likely sulk. It completely disappears by Summer meaning that other plants can grow in the space where it was.

SAXIFRAGE - LATIN NAME SAXIFRAGA - "LONDON PRIDE" 38 POINTS >**

Early into flower and this very small perennial is liked by young Spring hoverflies.

SAGE - LATIN NAME - SALVIA NEMOROSA "OSTFRIESLAND" "CARADONA" TYPICAL FLOWERING PERIOD 10/06—20/07 SYMBOLS >>>**

MAX POINTS SCORED 60 SMALL PERENNIAL

The subject of many a compulsive buy at the garden centre this plant has deep beautiful blue spikes of flowers. However its requirements are free draining soil, with moisture until it is well established. So don't bother if you are on clay if you cannot improve the soil drainage. Flowering in early June, this is a comparatively early plant into flower but if it does not like where you planted it, then it may not come back. The related half hardy sage can be seen in Chapter 12.

SKIMMIA JAPONICA TYPICAL FLOWERING PERIOD 01/04—01/05 SYMBOLS >>> 38

Requires acid soil, liked by early honeybees emerging from the hives. Male variety, ask for female plants for berries. Expensive small shrub. £20—40. Very shade tolerant.

PHOTINIA – LATIN NAME PHOTINIA "RED ROBIN"

TYPICAL FLOWERING PERIOD 25/05 - 20/06

SYMBOLS >>> MAX POINTS SCORED 57 LARGE SHRUB**

Photinia   "Red Robin" blooms with glorious, large, white, flowers which are of great benefit to insects. However this is normally bought as a hedging plant for its bright, red new leaves and cut back hard each year to produce that result. But this stops the plant being floriferous.   Insects will much appreciate you leaving this unpruned. I am sure you can do without some red leaves!

MEADOW RUE - LATIN NAME THALICTRUM FLAVUM

TYPICAL FLOWERING PERIOD 28/05—02/07

SYMBOLS >>>#~ MAX POINTS SCORED 79 MEDIUM SIZED PERENNIAL**

Thalictrums are naked flowers. Naked buttercups to be precise. Most other plants have petals and attractive colours, this just has the "business end" of the reward for insects. This makes the fluffy clouds of flowers vulnerable to heavy rain washing pollen away. In fact this plant is a design for wind pollination. However, pollinators are still interested but have to effectively fly at the flower to collect the reward. It is something to observe how different insects achieve this whether by "dive bombing" or trying to land somewhere with no effective landing strip! Bumblebees look very clumsy on this plant.

Thalictrum aquilegifolium "Black Stockings" This is a popular variety which can grow to 1.5 metres in a quarter shady border. Honey bees absolutely love this plant (picture below) I also like black stockings.

Thalictrum aquilegifolium "Thundercloud" is a long established variety and a safe bet.

There are also varieties in white which I find flower slightly less impressively though "White Cloud" is good.

Thalictrum flavum Glaucum. Flowers slightly earlier than the above plant with lovely light creamy yellow blooms. Also popular with bees and hoverflies.

Thalictrum delavayi

Avoid, cultivars such as **"Hewitts Double"** which did not score well in my research as the flowers do not offer much to insects.

TOP TIP

Thalictrum do not bloom for long, however if you combine flavum and aquilegifolium in the same area the bees will treat it as one longer flowering plant. If you plant around the edge of the plant with Aquilegia you will get an area of similar foliage which will look stunning in May and June. Also planting Purple Loosestrife next to Thalictrum makes a good waterside picture though go for a well behaved loosestrife variety. (See the article later on in this book).

PITTISPORNUM - LATIN NAME PITTISPORNUM TENUIFOLIUM

TYPICAL FLOWERING PERIOD 20/05—19/06

SYMBOLS >>~~~ POINTS SCORED 59 LARGE SHRUB

Small chocolate brown flowers appear between the leaves and are loved by insects that don't frequent gardens often. Wood wasps, (these do NOT sting) very small solitary bees and other strange but lovely "critters" visit mine! The best varieties are the most hardy so **Pittispornum tenuifolium** (pictured above) is the one to pick, described as a large shrub or small tree. **"Irene Patterson"** on the other hand is small, a slower growing foliage plant but as is often the case, the cultivation of such a plant seems to have reduced its ability to flower every year and to attract insects.

RED CAMPION - LATIN NAME SILENE DIOICA - NATIVE

TYPICAL FLOWERING PERIOD 15/05—10/06

SYMBOLS >>>#* MAX POINTS SCORED 57 SMALL PERENNIAL

It is a potential food plant of the Sandy and Twin Spotted Carpet, Campion, Lychnis and Rivulet Moth in its wild and native form. Campion likes a moist soil and a woodland edge situation. You should find that bees and butterflies visit this plant.

GRANNY'S BONNETS

LATIN NAME AQUILEGIA

TYPICAL FLOWERING PERIOD

03/05—14/06 SYMBOLS >>>*~ POINTS SCORED 61 SMALL PERENNIAL

A cottage garden favourite with a huge number of plants available in all colours. To try and avoid confusion when you buy, here is a list of some good ones for both appearances and for the insects!

Aquilegia "Georgia" is one new variety from the "State Series" with dark red and white flowers. Bees and plant enthusiasts do like this. **"Florida"** and **"Colorado"** are also recommended.

The "Songbird" series is also suitable for insects including plants such as **"Bunting"** and **"Chaffinch"**.

The more traditional "wild" form is **Aquilegia vulgaris** which is a short lived perennial which will self seed around with slightly smaller flowers. A long flowering period with the attention of interested bumblebees, who sometimes eat through the back of the plant to obtain easier access to the nectar and pollen. This plant is pictured above on 24th May, and comes in various colours, as you can see.

Whilst at a garden centre, steer clear of Aquilegia plants with frills and spurs and other bred "improvements" which obscure or reduce the amount of nectar and pollen available. Avoid **"Nora Barlow"**, **"Clementine Summer Rose"** or other **"Clementine"** varieties. Avoid anything with **"Winky"** in the name or anything else if it is a flouncy, double flower. They offer little to insects.

ROCK ROSE - LATIN NAME HELIANTHEMUM

TYPICAL FLOWERING PERIOD 01/05—15/06 SYMBOLS >>>*

POINTS SCORED 71 SMALL PERENNIAL

Relatively early flowering, this attracts the first hoverflies of the season who like to hang out beside the plant. It is also a pretty good bee plant. "**Wisley Primrose**" is the best for vigour and for a longer flowering period. The red, orange pink and white plants are all lovely but have fewer flowers. Look for flowering stems with many more flowers to come down the stem when buying as even individual plants vary in how floriferous they are. In a sunny spot , sprawling over a wall or path edge, this is a fantastic plant to have with a long flowering period. Recommended plants as follows...

"**Wisley Primrose**" (Light Yellow) "**The Bride**" (White) are the best plants. They flower for longest and appear more attractive to insects

"**Ben Mohr**" (Orange) "**Ben Phada**" (Yellow and Orange) "**Fire Dragon**" (Reddish) are good colourful varieties that perform well.

Avoid "**Amabile Plenum**" or "**Cerise Queen**" which has double flowers.

Helianthemum nummularium is the Native Rock Rose (Yellow) The foodplant of the **Brown Argus, Green Hairstreak** and the rare **Silver-studded Blue butterfly.**

CURRANT BUSH - LATIN NAME RIBES

TYPICAL FLOWERING PERIOD   15/03 - 20/04 SYMBOLS >>> 38 POINTS

Scores well with early bees and bumblebees "**King Edward VII**" and "**Elkingtons White**" are good plants for bees and easy to grow.

However they do not do much for the rest of the year looking somewhat ordinary which is the only downside to a plant that makes a good early contribution.

THE DIVA AWARD

BOTTLE BRUSH - LATIN NAME CALLISTEMON

TYPICAL FLOWERING PERIOD 01/05—01/06 SYMBOLS >>>>**

POINTS SCORED 70 MEDIUM SHRUB

Fancy a Diva? Yes? This beautiful plant, often seen at garden centres is worth the effort for bees, but you will need to meet its requirements, STRICTLY. Remember it is your favourite pop "Diva" in plant form, beautiful but demanding!

Firstly, neutral or acid compost only. Secondly, best grown in a pot. Thirdly, if you are in a hard or alkaline water area, water with rain water only. Chalk kills it, even one watering of alkaline tap water. Fourth, this will happily grow in Australia as a hedge, so if you are in Devon you might just about get it through Winter by leaving it outside, but safer bringing into a conservatory or protecting with fleece. The plant above is growing in Italy. Finally, buy **Incana** or **Citrinus** which are the most hardy, from the local market for about £10, garden centres may charge £80 for the same plant!

You can almost see the smile on the faces of the bumblebees that visit this plant. But if you grow Red Hot Pokers, you can get a similar result, however nothing is quite as rewarding as success with a plant like this. Its up to you and good luck!

41

SKULLCAP—LATIN NAME—SCUTELLARIA ALTISSIMA

TYPICAL FLOWERING PERIOD 10/05 –20/6   SYMBOLS >>>> POINTS 50

A good wildlife plant does not have to have large flowers. This is quite under the radar, small blue flowers on a plant up to 40 centimetres in height. You would probably only notice it is being visited by bumblebees, rather than the flowers. A perfect plant if you are not into showy things. Will self seed so is easy to build up a large clump. Can invade but is easy to pull up where not wanted. Will grow without much attention in a well drained sunny position but I have also had success in partial shade.

CORAL BELLS - LATIN NAME HEUCHERA

TYPICAL FLOWERING PERIOD VARIES—TYPICALLY 03/05—20/07

SYMBOLS >>>~ POINTS SCORED 79 SMALL PERENNIAL**

Heuchera often have a whole plant area devoted to them in garden centres. They are grown for the range of foliage colour available but the tiny flowers on slender stalks are rather better for bees and hoverflies than the small stature of the plant suggests. Every year new types come to the fore which means that, of any plants in this book, this is the one you must pick at the garden centre when in flower. Look for bees on the plant, and look for signs of new flowering stalks as well as the existing ones.

I think you should avoid the dodgy foliage colours of **"Key Lime Pie"** (yellow green foliage and not known for its flowers) and anything that looks like it is already dead (some have brown foliage!)

However, most other Heucheras flower well even **"Marmalade"** with rusty orange foliage (pictured opposite page) is reported as being good for honey bees. I recommend some of the deep red varieties and also those such as **"Paris",** which is red with icing style shading and rose pink flowers which are this year still out in October and **"Midnight Rose"** with dark red foliage and splashes of lighter pink flower well.

Some are shade tolerant for part of the day whereas others like the sun. Look at the label as they all have different characters. This plant is an illustration you can have enough choice of insect beneficial plants in your garden to make any selection other than that completely irrelevant. There is a Heuchera for everyone that will please the insects and also please you! ♥ Common Carder Bee Bombus pascourum

OXEYE DAISY - LATIN NAME LEUCANTHEMUM VULGARE

TYPICAL FLOWERING PERIOD

03/05—14/06 SYMBOLS >>>##POINTS SCORED 80 SMALL PERENNIAL**

Ox-eye daisies brighten up fields and meadows in May and are good plants for bees hoverflies early season butterflies and moths. This is available as **Leucanthemum vulgare** described in Garden Centres as a wild flower. It will grow well in a lawn situation and does not need good soil to succeed but does need moisture.

As usual, there are more "bred" varieties. I like **"May Queen"** which is an old variety and closely related to the wild plant. **"Silver Spoons"** is entertaining as it has the same nectar and pollen, but spidery petals which have the shape of a spoon on the end. I'll let you judge on whether that is a good thing or not!

KNAPWEED —CENTAUREA MONTANA

TYPICAL FLOWERING PERIOD 12/06—14/7

SYMBOLS /POINTS SCORED >># 56 MONTANA >>>##** 88**

MACROCEPHALA (FLOWERS 20/7—20/08) NIGRA >>>####* 99 points 29/05—05/08**

The short perennial cornflower pictured above) **Centaurea montana is** great for bees and an easy plant to grow. There are other related plants such as **"John Coutts" (Centaurea dealbata)**. Avoid **"Jordy"** as black flowers are unlikely to be noticed by insects.

The taller **Centaurea macrocephala** needs well drained soil and a bit of fussing to succeed. This is a good plant for insects including small beetles. **Centaurea nigra** is a native purple wild flower (see the meadow section) a top butterfly plant which scores 99 points.

All plants have short flowering periods in my experience but they are easy (mostly) to grow which is a redeeming feature.

HERRINGBONE COTONEASTER – LATIN NAME COTONEASTER HORIZONTALIS

TYPICAL FLOWERING PERIOD

15/05—01/06 SYMBOLS >>>>#* POINTS SCORED 60 SMALL SHRUB

♥ HONEY BEE APIS MELLIFERA

A small shrub which truly brings all the honey bees to the yard. It's a real shame that the flowering period is not longer, it is only a few weeks at the most. This negative is helped by the fact it has berries in Autumn which are loved by the birds especially thrushes. Ultimately it spreads but is never more than a metre high.

DANDELION - (LATIN NAME CREPIS) SYMBOLS >>>*#

FLOWERS 01/04—15/5 61 POINTS

♥ RED MASON BEE OSMIA BICORNIS

This is probably already around for free rather than paying for one at the garden centre. Dandelions have a place in a wildlife garden as they provide early season breakfast for solitary bees and butterflies (sometimes from February onwards)

Not many visitors can be expected initially, but those that do will be grateful to you. It is a preference plant for insects.

Top Tip

Pull them out (including all the roots) where you don't want them but dead head the flowers when the yellow starts to fade, on those you want to keep. You will have a clump, where you want them to be though inevitably there will be invaders from elsewhere.

PEONY—LATIN NAME- PAEONIA LATIFOILIA

TYPICAL FLOWERING PERIOD 08/05—1/06 SYMBOLS >>>##

POINTS SCORED 57   MEDIUM PERENNIAL

Peonies are some of the most fabulous flowers you will ever see though the majority are doubles which offer nothing to insects. There are a number of single flowered plants which flower briefly but offer huge flowers which are appreciated by foraging bees in May. They can be tricky to grow though I have some in my garden that seem to need little attention. **"White Wings"** is one to start with (pictured above). They need a well drained soil with plenty of nutrients.

THE SUMMER MEADOW

Pictured above the peak of **Ox Eye Daisies** at **Sissinghurst** in Kent in June. This is a place known for its support of butterflies and for its beautiful meadow and is well worth visiting. You can also visit Winston Churchills' butterfly garden at **Chartwell** which also has a managed meadow for butterflies. It is a little known fact that Churchill was one of the first wildlife gardeners having planted borders exclusively for them. Seeing butterflies around his place helped him with his depression. Both locations are National Trust properties.

If you are lucky enough to have a large area of lawn, it is possible to leave some of it uncut so that it becomes (eventually) a meadow.

CREATING A MEADOW

1) Allowing existing plants such as **Clover, Horseshoe Vetch and Hawksbeard** to bloom is a first step. Grasses are also attractive when they go to seed. You may be surprised what is already in your lawn and it may save you money actually buying what you already have!

2) Sow a seed mix, often sold as a "meadow mix" though check that the contents are native plants. In this section, we are NOT interested in exotics.

3)   The meadow should be cut back after flowering early August. Leave collecting the cuttings for a couple of weeks to allow seeds to fall back into the soil.

4)   Reduce fertility in the soil by removing cuttings for the first few years after the meadow has been started. This reduces the vigour of grasses to allow more flowers to appear.

5)   Planting actual plants in the lawn is a way of being specific to insect requirements especially where a plant is stated as a native. Garden centres do sell plug plants which can be put in the lawn in September. But this is a much more expensive option than using a seed mix, or allowing nature to decide what will be in your meadow, which is actually of no cost at all.

A selection of plants (perennial unless otherwise stated) for growing in grass are

Field Scabious Knautia arvensis **Knapweed,** Centaurea nigra

Wild Carrot, Daucus carota (annual)

Clover (Red / White) Trifolium pratense / Trifolium repens

Horseshoe vetch (food plant of **Chalkhill** and **Adonis Blue butterflies)**

Ox Eye Daisy Leucanthemum vulgare

Yarrow Achillea millefolium

Ladies Bedstraw Galium verum

Tufted Vetch Vicia cracca

Perforate St Johns Wort Hypericum perforatum

Meadow Cranesbill Geranium pratense and **Toadflax** Linaria vulgaris

Wild Marjoram, Origanum vulgare

Birds Foot Trefoil Lotus corniculatus

Vipers Bugloss Echium vulgare (biennial)

Flanders Poppy. Papaver rhoeas (annual)

Grasses try "**Yorkshire Fog and "Red Fescue"**

Avoid **"Fox and Cubs"** Pilosella aurantiaca which does not attract insects. Allow the very common **Smooth Hawksbeard,** Crepis capillaris instead. Avoid any seed mix with **Thistle** as most types are very invasive and problematic.

Cowslips and Crocus can provide the early shift of flowers in a meadow.

Using mostly perennial plants means more initial cost overall. However annual plants may not self seed if the fertility of the soil is too high. A key feature of a meadow is to leave it undisturbed as much as possible. If one plant takes over, just dig it out, don't use any weedkiller, you could kill off the insects you want to help. If you know of pernicious weeds in the lawn before setting up the meadow, deal with them before it is established.

A meadow is a habitat, more than the sum of its individual parts.

Pictured above is a recently planted meadow with **Ladies Bedstraw, Knapweed,Birds Foot Trefoil** and other species such as **Field Scabious** and **Achillea** waiting in the wings. The right grasses (see chapter 9) are also planted as food plants for butterflies.

This meadow was simply teeming with insect life. Butterflies, bees, crickets, hoverflies. Such an inspirational message of hope here. We can reverse the decline in biodiversity, but we need more farmers and gardeners to help insects with the plants that they plant. But just think how great it would be to see more of this.

WHITE DEADNETTLE—LAMIUM ALBUM (NATIVE WILD FLOWER)

TYPICAL FLOWERING PERIOD   10/04—18/5 SYMBOLS >>>>*

POINTS SCORED 60 - SMALL PERENNIAL

If you are planting a wildlife garden this is an essential inclusion as it is a preference plant for all early bumblebees. It likes disturbed soil such as that above rabbit burrows, sun for most of the day but also moisture and fertility. There is also a red deadnettle, nowhere near as good in attracting insects as the White.

Cultivated and easily grown alternatives such as **"White / Red Nancy"** and **"Shell Pink"** are well worth trying. **"Pink Chablis"** and the native score best with insects. Be careful with others as some plants are bred just for the foliage, and can be shy to flower. For emerging White Tailed and Buff Tailed Bumblebees, and rarer species as well, this is a top preference plant.

Avoid **Lamiastrum galeobdolon** a superficially similar plant with yellow flowers which is dangerously invasive.

BROOM - LATIN NAME CYTISUS

TYPICAL FLOWERING PERIOD   07/04 —09/05 SYMBOLS >>> 38

♥   EARLY BUMBLEBEE BOMBUS PRATORUM

Shrub for dry sunny situation Cytisus praecox "Warminster" is the best variety. I am yet to see much on anything other than "Warminster". The plant scores less due to the sporadic nature of the interest from insects but some years is popular.

BLADDER SENNA - LATIN NAME COLUTEA

TYPICAL FLOWERING PERIOD 28/03—20/05

03/05—14/06 SYMBOLS >>>*~ POINTS SCORED 63 SMALL CLIMBING PLANT OR SHRUB

Its not exactly a famous plant. However it is found along railways as an escapee from gardens and I have it in my garden, though I did not plant it. It is early into flower, and unlike **Forsythia**, which offers nothing to bees, this is a very good bee plant and at a stretch could be planted instead of **Forsythia,** it's a bit more subtle with its yellow tones but still a pleasant sight when in flower.

You will rarely see it at garden centres, it will most likely be on a small trellis or sold as a shrub or climber but is definitely worth investing in if you see it.

Above: Alstroemeria comes in different foliage and flower colours all with "bling" turned up to 11

PRINCESS LILY - LATIN NAME ALSTROEMERIA

TYPICAL FLOWERING PERIOD 10/06—05/09 >>>*

SYMBOLS POINTS SCORED 62 SMALL HALF HARDY PERENNIAL

I classify this as a "Diva" though my garden just does not suit them being cold, with clay soil and few areas of high sunshine. So don't be put off if you have a sunny garden with good soil with gritty drainage.

There are some more hardy varieties available and you will see them at garden centres being visited by bumblebees as in the picture above. The soft foliage is loved by slugs however.

PLANTING ADVICE

A tender perennial, so this may get through your local Winter in the south half of the UK with a mulch of material above it and planted at a depth of 6 inches. Recommended **Alstroemerias** include **"Indian Summer"** and **"Summer Breeze"** (pictured previous page) which has darker foliage. **"Ligtu"** Hybrids also have a lot of vigour which means they may be a little more tolerant if the conditions are not 100% what they want. Best bought from specialists.

VIPERS BUGLOSS LATIN ECHIUM VULGARE

TYPICAL FLOWERING PERIOD 10/06-20/07

SYMBOLS >>>>##~* POINTS SCORED 96 SMALL ANNUAL

❤ WHITE TAILED BUMBLEBEE BOMBUS LUCORUM

Vipers Bugloss flowers in the "June lull" This is one of the very best bumblebee plants though I have always found it difficult in my clay soil.

It happily grows in well drained chalk grassland such as that near Box Hill in Surrey where it provides splashes of the deepest royal blue. It grows even better on stones and gravel at the RSPB reserve near Dungeness, Kent.

"Vulgare" is the wild (biennial) UK Native variety. You can buy seeds of the annual **"Blue Bedder"** and plants of **"Red Feathers"** which are easy to grow in gritty conditions but only expect one year of colour from these plants.

Echium Pininana is one of the best bee plants of all 2 metres high but easy only if you live by the coast in Devon, or Cornwall. Needs to grow in grit, in full sun. Known as **"Tower of Jewels"** this biennial/triennial actually becomes a tower of bees! (scores 80 points).

PHACELIA is a similar annual to **Vipers Bugloss** and every bit as good as Bugloss. It is sometimes grown as a crop in fields and is very much recommended if you want to try a bed of mixed annuals. **82 points >>>##~***

CRIMSON LOOSESTRIFE

LATIN NAME LYSIMACHIA ATROPURPEREA ("BEAUJOLAIS")

TYPICAL FLOWERING PERIOD 20/05—05/07

SYMBOLS >>>#*~

POINTS SCORED 62

I've seen this beautiful plant sold as a biennial, and a perennial. Perennial? No way!

This makes it expensive potentially but it is a good plant for bees with a very long flowering period. It likes moist, well drained soil and some TLC and then it might come back next year.

Other flowers in the genus Lysimachia are less attractive to insects apart **from Lysimachia ciliata "Firecandle"** a bronze plant with yellow flowers that does attract some bees but not scoring as highly as "Beaujolais".

LEOPARD PLANT—LIGULARIA

TYPICAL FLOWERING PERIOD 10/07—01/08

SYMBOLS >>>##~**
POINTS SCORED 76

These plants have leaves attractive to slugs and are best placed by a pond. This is not just because the habit of towering flowers looks right in that situation but to give the maximum chance for slugs to be eaten by frogs emerging from the pond. Some varieties such as **"Othello"** (orange flowers) are more prone to such attacks than others. I have found **"The Rocket" (pictured left)** to grow reliably for several years now. Once established the plant provides many yellow flowers that are loved by most insects. They like a damp situation with avoidance of mid-day sun and watering at the end of a hot Summer day.

THE POISONOUS PAGES—DEADLY PLANTS FOR INSECTS

There are plants you should not have in your garden for bees, and some common plants that can even kill bees. Check if you have any of these about your area.

SOPHORA MICROPHYLLA "SUN KING"

This gives bees an LSD style trip from which they never recover. This plant blooms early, is very attractive to bees and is especially poisonous in cooler conditions. It should never be sold (but still is) as it often kills bumblebees, and was subject to research as long ago as 1972. I've unwittingly witnessed this occurrence first hand, dying bumblebees on the ground in February to April but none when the plant was gone. (New Zealand Agricultural Research P. G. Clinch, T. Palmer-Jones & I. W. Forster).

SOLANUM NIGRUM—BLACK NIGHTSHADE
Toxic to bees and also a wild native to the UK.

RHODODENDRON SPECIES

Beekeepers keep hives closed until these plants have finished flowering as the plant in many forms is poisonous to hive bees, (and reported for solitary bees, mining bees too) causing gradual death. Sterile plants are safe. Ponticum, occidentale, macrophyllum, albiflorum are said to contain grayanotoxins, the poison that causes the problem. Honey produced with this is not suitable for human consumption either. Also applies to **AZALEA.**

DATURA—ANGELS TRUMPET. Used to be sold more often as a patio plant. This contains all sorts of toxins and these can cause death to young bees in the hive, fed from the plant.

BOG ROSEMARY This will cause death to bees and contaminate honey.

RICINUS—CASTOR BEAN. Planted as an annual, often for its red foliage. The plant can produce bio diesel. This is so toxic it leads to death to honey bees. Seeds would kill you too. Plantations in Brazil will only increase bee deaths there.

OLEANDER

This is a very toxic plant and is often planted in warmer climes. Eat it and you will die. It does not offer anything to bees other than toxins which can cause a hive to suffer casualties. **KALMIA** is similar and causes stomach problems for humans if honey is obtained from the plant. Often seen at garden centres.

YELLOW JESSAMINE (GELSEMIUM SEMPERVIRENS)

State flower of California and absolutely fatal to broods of honey bees which it attracts with a sweet, deadly scent. How do Californians feel about this?

CAMILIA SINENSIS—The "Tea plant" kills bees and leads to brood death in overseas tea plantations according to one study in Darang, India (Sharma et al 1986) More study on plants such as this is needed. Don't feed bees with tea, is my advice… though why would you, really?

VERATRUM FALSE HELLEBORE

Pollinated by bees and other insects which it kills in the process, this extremely poisonous plant is hard to grow and to flower but has been available widely in garden centres. Inhaling the pollen can cause breathing difficulties in us humans too.

ASCLEPIAS—Often sold at garden centres, this appears to make bees drunk, but there is not a study out there to comfirm whether this does any more specific harm, the plant is very much liked by insects. It contains chemicals best avoided.

STARGAZER LILY (LILIUM) Poisonous to cats and also causes death for bees. Do I need to say any more?

There needs to be more study on other plants, **HEMEROCALLIS** (fatal for cats) is a close relative to the Lily above but there is nothing to suggest it is fatal for bees. However studies into **LUPIN** by the British Ecological Society show that fewer offspring are produced by bumblebees that forage on this plant. What other plants are there that could be causing a similar problem?

So not only do some Garden Centres sell plants drenched with chemicals, they actually sell some plants that kill bees, though I guess many will be unaware of this. We should be changing our attitude to such plants given the decline in insect populations and we should be influencing the type of plants sold by garden centres.

ANGELICA GIGAS Hello.... I'm just checking you are still paying attention! Yes? The plant above is **ANGELICA GIGAS** and is loved by wasps. This was at a garden centre, but nobody was buying! There were 25 wasps on just one flower on the plant above, and 4 flowers. I wouldn't fancy taking the wasps to the checkout myself...

If you plant **ANGELICA SYLVESTRIS,** a related plant, and a herb, which flowers in the Spring and Summer you will help bees, hoverflies and butterflies, rather than specifically wasps. This just illustrates why you do need to be careful to obtain the RIGHT plants from this book. Even closely related plants such as these Angelicas can produce different results.

CHAPTER 5 —
THE BEST PLANTS JULY TO OCTOBER

We now move firmly through the Summer and on until Autumn.

THE FAMILY OF MALVACEAE

LATIN NAME LAVATERA, ALCEA, MALVA

Lets talk about **Malvaceae** otherwise known as the Mallow family. They are related plants, perennials, biennials and shrubs. They have similar flowers and are all fantastic plants for bees.

HOLLYHOCK - LATIN NAME ALCEA RUGOSA ALCEA ROSEA

TYPICAL FLOWERING PERIOD 20/06—30/07 (RUGOSA) SYMBOLS >>>*

POINTS SCORED 73   LARGE PERENNIAL

Small Alcea plants are very prone to slug damage however where **Alcea rugosa** seeds itself in cracks in pavements, the plant beats the slugs (as shown in the picture right) and blooms earlier than **Alcea rosea** itself when given such conditions. **Alcea rosea** is found in many colours as a "single" flowering plant Avoid the large number of frilly double flowers available that offer nothing to any insects.

MALLOW - LATIN NAME   LAVATERA

TYPICAL FLOWERING PERIOD 20/06—20/08

SYMBOLS >>>#***
POINTS SCORED 98
MEDIUM / LARGE SHRUB

Mallows are large shrubs with grey green foliage. They dislike Winter wet, or too much shade and respond well to warm sunshine. Despite pollen and nectar being somewhat sticky, bumblebees do love this plant.

Pictured above. **Lavatera "Burgundy Wine"**

The Tree Mallow **Lavatera arborea** is a seaside plant, also loved by bees

MALLOW - LATIN NAME MALVA SYLVESTRIS MAURITIANA

TYPICAL FLOWERING PERIOD   20/06—30/07 SYMBOLS >>>>***

POINTS SCORED 80   MEDIUM PERENNIAL

Malva sylvestris "Mauritania" easily grown from seed and produces flowers that bees go crazy for, you just have to be patient with its habit of leaves that look poor or suffer from rust after flowering, a habit it shares with **Alcea** plants.

Lavatera clementii "Rosea" (Rose) and **"Barnsley"** (Pink/White). The largest shrubs (2x2 metres) and the easiest and most tolerant of frost or Winter wet.

Lavatera olbia "Red Rum" (Deep Rose and pictured above) 1.2 metres by 1.2 metres, a smaller plant. It actually grows in my garden in a more shady position than it would ideally like, but it has been there 8 years. **"Burgundy Wine"** is larger but similar. The more unusual and bi-coloured the types of Lavatera are, the less satisfactory the length of flowering period and overall performance. I put in this category **Lavatera maritima** (it grows well in California, clue... the UK is not California) **Lavatera clementii "Songbird"** (White) **Malva "Primley Blue"**. Any variety with smaller flowers or, as I found, a plant with white flowers that turn pink, is a pale imitation of the original plant. We have to have the best performers here only, otherwise our insects will be disappointed when they visit our gardens.

TOP TIP

Typically, Lavateras are Winter losses, getting too wet or cold or getting to the end of a 4 or 5 year average life span. Take cuttings from a non flowering shoot in midSummer as an insurance policy. Clip back after flowering to promote new growth and leave that over Winter as frost protection.

FALSE SPIRAEA— LATIN NAME SORBARIA ARBOREA

TYPICAL FLOWERING PERIOD 01/07—10/08 SYMBOLS >>>>***~~~POINTS SCORED 100 - LARGE SHRUB

Seek out a specialist nursery for this plant which is a large shrub but without the spreading tendency of relative **Sorbaria sorbifolia** and its ilk. It attracts a great range of insects to its huge, fluffy, clouds of bloom and It has a slight odour which attracts flies and wood wasps. This is always bustling with insects when the blooms are out. After flowering, immediately cut back a third of the shoots to about 1.5 metres in height, to promote good flowering next year, and to avoid it getting too tall, as it can top 5 metres left unpruned!

CATMINT — LATIN NAME NEPETA FAASINII "SIX HILLS GIANT"

TYPICAL FLOWERING PERIOD 08/06—20/07

SYMBOLS >>>>***~

POINTS SCORED 91 SMALL PERENNIAL

It used to be that my cat Holly (pictured above) ate this plant to the ground before I could evaluate the insects that visited. Sadly, I lost my cat during the last year.

But my loss is the gain of the bees and hoverflies that flock to this small perennial. But I can't help thinking about my little companion of 12 years as I look at this plant. It may be that your own cat will eat this plant before insects arrive. **Lavendula intermedia** is an alternative plant if this happens.

ELECAMPANE - LATIN NAME INULA

TYPICAL FLOWERING PERIOD   25/06—22/07

SYMBOLS   HOOKERI >>>####**~   HELENIUM >>>>###**~

INULA HOOKERI 98 - SMALL PERENNIAL POINTS SCORE

INULA MAGNIFICA 99 - LARGE PERENNIAL

Inula hookeri has beautiful flowers beloved by butterflies and most bees. It is best put in an area where its vigour is appreciated, in among other plants it is easy to remove if it does wander a bit too much!

Inula helenium is a stately plant 2-3 metres high with large yellow daisy flowers.

Telekia speciosa is similar and also available from more specialist nurseries. Both of these larger plants dominate an area, and they are best in a corner, or cut back after flowering which allows neighbouring plants a chance to recover.

"Magnifica" is larger and more coarse and very attractive to bees. This is a wild garden plant. All Inula are good for insects though **Inula hookerii** is the choice if you do not have much room. They tolerate some (but not too much) shade and are very easy to look after.

PENSTEMON - LATIN NAME - PENSTEMON

TYPICAL FLOWERING PERIOD (GARNET)   25/06—10/09 SYMBOLS >>>>**#

POINTS SCORED 91 - MEDIUM PERENNIAL

💚 GARDEN BUMBLEBEE BOMBUS HORTORUM

I have grown several varieties in my cold garden on a hill. **"Blackbird"** a deep purple, lasted a few years and **"Raven"** which is similar and **"Sour Grapes",** a blue white plant, didn't last long. There are many others which promise so much.

But it is **"Andenken an Friedrich Hahn"** still known (thank goodness) as **Penstemon "Garnet"** which persists after 10 years, and the coldest of Winters in my garden. As the longest flowering, this is the best for bees. It is also very easy to propagate, simply put some cuttings in moist well drained soil, or plant a piece of root. It can spread quickly when happy, but this just gives you an opportunity to try it in other areas of the garden by division. One specific finding of my research is how large the number of red or near red flowers that are favoured. Bees are supposed to find this colour hard to see but they manage to find it where it counts for them! Bumblebees are one of the most frequent visitors to Penstemon.

PLANTING ADVICE

Leave growth without cutting back over Winter, as the top growth protects the rest of the plant against frost.   Dead head the flower stems and they will keep blooming for longer. Incorporate some grit in soil for drainage. This plant loves growing over a wall, where it may spread well (see my picture of **"Garnet"** above)

KNOTWEED - LATIN NAME - PERSICARIA

TYPICAL FLOWERING PERIOD   15/07—15/08 SYMBOLS >>>**~~~

POINTS SCORED 96 - LARGE PERENNIAL

♥ VESPULA VULGARIS—COMMON WASP

Bistort (Bistorta officinalis) is described elsewhere so this page deals with all the other **Persicarias** often described as Knotweed. These have a wider range of results for insects than any other plant group I have studied. **Persicaria amplexicaulis** varieties such as **"Firetail "** are long flowering and loved by honey bees. I must warn you it is unusually adored by wasps too. I would plant this away from your back door as a result!

This attractiveness to insects should be the case when you see the plant at the garden centre. Just to make it complicated, very similar looking plants may also be sold as **"Firetail"** which don't attract insects which is why you must buy this one when in flower and when there are insect visitors to the local garden centre.

The score here is for the **Persicaria amplexicaulis** plants only. Avoid **Persicaria affinis** and **Persicaria polymorpha.** This latter is a large, stately plant with bright white flowers which is one of the most useless "wildlife plants" available. So here I go... disagreeing with the "perfect pollinator" label it sometimes receives. It attracts as many insects as a brick over many years of study.

Other Persicarias also get a bit too demanding of room too so stick with **Persicaria amplexicaulis "Firetail"** which only gradually fills up an area and is recommended for partially shaded situations. Pictured above.

THE ANNUAL CORNER

Annuals are plants that live one year and they may also be half hardy plants that are only planted for a year.

COSMOS - LATIN NAME - COSMOS BIPINNATUS

TYPICAL FLOWERING PERIOD   05/06—10/10

SYMBOLS >>>>##***~

POINTS SCORED 132 - SMALL ANNUAL

💚 BUFF TAILED BUMBLEBEE BOMBUS TERRESTRIS

Mixes such as **"Sonata Mix"** and just plain **"Carmine"** (pictured above) are busy with insects all day long. Avoid short (less than 14 centimetres) or "fluted" types and notice how large the centre of the flower is in the plant above for providing pollen and nectar. This is key to the best forms of this plant, and the many dozens of flowers each plant produces in a season is a particular feature, this is a real "giver". This needs sun, a well drained soil and protection from slugs when it is a youngster. Better to plant a larger plant in the garden, then watch a little plug plant vanish courtesy of a local slug. Needs well drained sandy soil and deadhead on a daily basis to promote flowers, and collect some seed to grow next year.

CALIFORNIAN POPPY - LATIN NAME - ESCHSCHOLZIA CALIFORNICA

TYPICAL FLOWERING PERIOD   01/07—30/08

SYMBOLS >>**~ POINTS SCORED 65 SMALL ANNUAL

The orange flowered plant (the wild original also stated to be "Orange King") will flower for longer and is more vigorous. Often féted as a wildlife plant, insects visit, but it will depend where you are how long they stay. I have recorded some good years with this plant and others not quite as good.

POACHED EGG PLANT - LATIN NAME - LIMNANTHES DOUGLASII

TYPICAL FLOWERING PERIOD 15/05—20/6 SYMBOLS >>>*~ POINTS SCORED 79 SMALL ANNUAL**

Good for bees and early hoverflies, but you need quite a few plants for this to be successful. Place this between other plants it will seed itself around. Can only be really grown from seed, sown in situ, where it is to grow.

POT MARIGOLD - LATIN NAME - CALENDULA OFFICINALIS

TYPICAL FLOWERING PERIOD 01/07—01/10 SYMBOLS >>>*

POINTS SCORED 100 SMALL ANNUAL

There is an urban myth that this plant repels bees. Not judging on the interest of honey bees in this plant and hoverflies love it too. The smell (which I consider to be fruity, not unpleasant) will repel greenfly and whitefly which is why it is planted with crops vulnerable to such things. Companion planting is infinitely preferable to pesticides and weed killers, so plant single marigolds around your vegetables or fruit as well as **Poached Egg Plants** and **Cosmos** and **Nasturtium.**

SUNFLOWER - LATIN NAME   HELIANTHUS ANNUUS

TYPICAL FLOWERING PERIOD   01/07—01/09 SYMBOLS >>>*

POINTS SCORED 61 LARGE ANNUAL

Fun for children (and adults!) to grow and a great plant for all bees, I have a (personal) preference for the perennial Sunflower over all due to its later flowering period.(described elsewhere)

But there is nothing better than the picture an annual sunflower creates and many types are available. Avoid ghastly double flowers such as **"Teddy Bear"** and "no pollen" alternatives that will not help insects at all. Instead go for the not too tall single varieties in various colours such as **"Lemon / Velvet Queen" "Firecracker" "Autumn Beauty" "Red Sun".** Some of these are branching plants which offer more flowers than the single stem single flower alternatives. **"Italian White"** and **"Moon walker"** did well in my trial.

CRANESBILL - LATIN NAME - GERANIUM

♥ TREE BUMBLEBEE—BOMBUS HYPNORUM

There are many different varieties of this hardy groundcover plant but guidance is needed to pick the best varieties for insects. Best described in a table of different types, which follows below.

Type	Symbols	Details	Comment
Geranium macrorrhizum (42 points)	>>>	Pink	Good for bees in early Summer
Geranium psilostemon "Patricia" (59 points)	>>>**	Rose Pink	Good for bees Early Summer
Geranium renardii	>>	White/ Purple	Shy flowering
Geranium pratense (Native 58 Points)	>>>**	Blue	Good for meadow planting
Geranium oxonianum such as "Claridge Druce"	>>	Pink/ Rose	Avoid ! Invasive! Seedlings!
Geranium clarkii "Kashmir White"	>>	White	
Geranium "Orion" or "Brookside"	>>>	Blue	Early Summer , old variety would be **"Johnsons Blue"**
Geranium "Rozanne (103 points)"	>>>##**	Purple Blue	Best plant for bees and for habit
Geranium "Mrs Kendall Clark"	>>>	White grey blue	Short flowering period
Geranium x Oxonianum "Wargrave Pink"	>>>	Pink	Traditional quickly spreading variety
Geranium "Ann Folkard"	>>	Pink	
Pelargoniums	Nil	Nil	Avoid these bedding plants also described as "Geraniums"

Left **Geranium "Rozanne"** and **below Geranium psilostemon "Patricia"** a variety of Armenian Cranesbill

Planting advice All plants benefit from cutting back after flowering. Where you have half shade, you can try the more vigorous varieties such as **Geranium "Macorrhizum"**. I would avoid the really rampant ones, I spend more time pulling up **"Claridge Druce"** than I do unwanted dandelions!

Otherwise they are forgiving, easy ground cover plants to grow and a must for success in shade.

Geranium psilostemon

GOATSBEARD - LATIN NAME - ARUNCUS

TYPICAL FLOWERING PERIOD 02/07—20/07 SYMBOLS >>>**

POINTS SCORED 50 MEDIUM PERENNIAL

This is a plant for a shaded position. Buy the standard version **Aruncus dioicus** for the longest and biggest flower spikes. This is also a European wild flower which I encountered in natural woodland in North Italy,

"Glasnevin" flowers less. **"Horatio"** flowers less than **"Glasnevin"** but it is a beautiful smaller plant that has the appearance of a fern and good Autumnal colours. So plant it if you would otherwise have planted a fern. it does more for wildlife than a fern! Avoid **Aruncus aethusifolius** with its little flowers of little value.

BUTTERFLY BUSH - BUDDLEIA

TYPICAL FLOWERING PERIOD 30/06—10/09 SYMBOLS >>>>####*~**

POINTS UP TO 138 (+) LARGE SHRUB

If you go into many woodland edges or hedgerows or along railways, (where plants are treated with herbicide, without thought for insects or wildlife) you will see the "wild" variety of light purple **Buddleia davidii (+)** identified by an orange eye to the purple flowers.

This is a large and long flowered plant and is very good for both bees and butterflies. It is classified as invasive, as ironically in open fields it has the capacity to destroy butterfly habitat whilst providing food for them. It destroys brickwork in paving or where it grows on a roof. So it is preferable to plant smaller cultivars from your local garden centre as stated below than rely on an unruly, natural, gift even if it is appreciated by so many insects.

All varieties of **Buddleia davidii**

"Buzz" a dwarf variety you can grow in a pot in various shades.

"Sugar Plum" grows 3—5 feet, smaller than most and floriferous. (+)

"White Profusion" is supra- attractive to moths. However I would suggest this is because you can see the moths on a bright white plant at night.   Not so easy on a dark purple plant. I'm still observing this plant to see what happens.

"Black Knight" For me the dark purple flowers are too dark but it is a good flowering variety. (+)

"Harlequin" Despite being variegated, this flowers and performs well and really stands out! It is about 2-3 metres tall when pruned. (+)

"Border Beauty" has rosy purple flowers and flowers for a long period. (+)

Avoid **"Pink Delight"** which flowers less, and has pink flowers that fade to mid brown, and look awful when that happens.

Maximum score of 138 is allocated to those with a (+) as above. However you may find the performances of plants vary, even so.

66

Other types—**Buddleia**

Buddleia alternifolia—Spring early Summer flowering, weeping, lilac, for a short period, attractive to earlier bees but not as good as **Buddleia davidii** varieties

Buddleia globosa, orange ball shaped flowers in early Summer. Definitely a good bee plant but grows very large for a small garden.

Buddleia provide nectar, but they are so large that there is always an argument to consider five different wildlife friendly plants to occupy the space one Buddleia would occupy.

CALAMINTH - LATIN NAME - CALAMINTHA

TYPICAL FLOWERING PERIOD 1/07 —20/09

SYMBOLS >>>>***###~~~~ POINTS 150 - SMALL PERENNIAL

♥ HONEY BEE - APIS MELLIFERA

This unassuming small plant is one of the best overall. It has a very long flowering period, takes up little room and is attractive to all beneficial pollinating insects. You can spend time working out what the "micro moths" are that visit, among many other things. It smells minty fresh not just if you rub the foliage between your fingers. On a hot day you can detect the scent easily. Not trumpeted much elsewhere, this is a fantastic plant. Grow as much of it as you can. Pictured above **Calamintha "Blue Cloud"** with light blue flowers. **"White Cloud"** is just as excellent.

Calamintha is not going to like anything other than growing over a wall, in full sun, It never does as well with some shade. I think you can see the situation it likes above. The rewards for fulfilling its requirements are rich. I advocate this in a hanging basket in a later chapter but you could also use it in a sunny windowbox.

GOLDEN ROD - LATIN NAME - SOLIDAGO CANADENSIS

TYPICAL FLOWERING PERIOD 20/07—31/08 SYMBOLS >>##~~~**

POINTS SCORED 101 - LARGE PERENNIAL (2 Metres high)

♥ HOVERFLY MYATHROPA FLOREA & GREENBOTTLE SPECIES

I remember my mum pulling out this plant completely when I was a teenager after we had it in the garden many years. "But you are robbing the bees of their breakfast" I said. This is a plant also for hoverflies and wood wasps. Greenbottles love it. I can hear the question "why help them?". They can't help being greenbottles, they still need food to survive. It is easy to feed off a **Solidago** if you are a insect, you just land, and stick out your tongue, like landing in a bowl of sweet custard. Have a look at your insect identification book and have fun trying to work out what the many insects that visit are. We must not judge what makes up biodiverse nature on appearance, everything has value and purpose. So let us not look down at anything, even greenbottles.

Of course a big negative is that this plant is a weed of wasteland , but it has been well behaved for 10 years in my garden. There is a way to keep it under control. Keep it hemmed in by rocks just below the surface is one piece of advice, if it looks like it should wander somewhere. Only plant in drier ground, not by water. Avoid **Solidaster** or smaller **Solidago**, they are poor alternatives with a lesser flowering period.

PLANTING TIPS

After flowering cut the plant down to the base. If you don't want unwanted seedlings or potentially to feed the birds. You can plant other plants that bloom early in the year at the base. I have Ajuga and Pulmonaria around mine.   Dig out the hard core of the plant periodically if is spreads too much. Its good on the edge of a lawn which hems it in if you mow the edge to where you want it to be.

LAMBS EARS - LATIN NAME— STACHYS LANATA

TYPICAL FLOWERING PERIOD 10/06—10/08 SYMBOLS >>>*

POINTS SCORED 50 - SMALL PERENNIAL

♥ Wool carder bee Anthidium manicatum will use the bluish grey, hairy leaves for its nest, but the flowers of this plant are super for all bees. However avoid varieties such as **"Big Ears"** (foliage and little flower) If in doubt buy in flower at the garden centre and look for good spikes of erect, woolly, clothed, pinky blue flowers. Must have a sunny position to succeed and it can be untidy, flop and look unappealing until established. It looks best crawling over a path edge in a place where it heats up, it will disappoint if placed in even some shade.

GERMANDER - LATIN NAME -TEUCRIUM

TYPICAL FLOWERING PERIOD 10/07—20/ 08 SYMBOLS >>>>###**

MAXIMUM POINTS SCORED 100

The perennial **Teucrium** is about a metre high and has spikes of purple flowers. Bumblebees and honey bees seek them out, to the extent that my neighbouring Lavender plant was not given half as much attention for a few weeks, which shows how much this plant is beloved. Two main varieties are **Teucrium hircanicum "Purple Tails"** (pictured above) and the smaller rockery plant **Teucrium chaemaedrys** (pictured left). My plants grow either right on the edge of the driveway or through a crack in a pavement. In other words, they like it hot with sun for most of the day. Once established, they are drought tolerant and will self seed nicely in abandoned corners.

Daucus carota (white) weaves through **Cosmos** and **Verbena bonariensis**

WILD CARROT - LATIN NAME - DAUCUS CAROTA

TYPICAL FLOWERING PERIOD 17/06—18/08 SYMBOLS ***~~~

POINTS SCORED 76 MEDIUM PERENNIAL UK NATIVE PLANT

This was a slow burner in my research, but eventually was found by a wide range of insects. It isn't a bee plant, or a butterfly plant in my experience. So this is a plant for the other insects. It needs protection from slugs initially but then spreads to provide flowers for at least two solid months. The single plant above was £1.99 at a garden centre so it gave good value, albeit for only one year.

If you have sensitive skin wear gloves when handling and note that it is not anywhere near as good to eat as a carrot, despite being called "carrot". We are dealing with insect food requirements here too, not yours! It may self seed the next year, so reduce the attractive "birds nests" that persist through Winter if concerned. In the USA this plant is a "noxious weed". The UK climate stops it getting to that stage.

It is a food plant for a widespread continental butterfly, the European swallowtail, but whilst some were found in one area of the South of the UK in 2014, it is not worth planting specifically for that.

LAVENDER - LATIN NAME - LAVANDULA

TYPICAL FLOWERING PERIOD HIDCOTE/ MUNSTEAD 17/06—18/08 / INTERMEDIA 15/07 - 15/09   SYMBOLS *###~~~ / INTERMEDIA >>>>####***~**

POINTS SCORED 98 /126 SMALL PERENNIAL

With Lavender, don't be tempted in a garden centre by breeding creations such as pink lavender, extra big lavender or variegated lavender. The "butterfly" types with a blob of foliage and a fancy top are less hardy and less effective for bees.

The best plants are the old favourites.   For bees, **Lavandula angustifolia "Hidcote"** provides a month of fabulous flowers for them as does **"Munstead"** (pictured above) and this is slightly taller. **Lavender x intermedia "Sussex"** flowers later and for at least a whole month extra. It attracts my local butterflies. In well drained soil, this should get through all but the most extreme of Winters.   This has taller grey blue flowers that stand clear and separate from the foliage. So I have that in my garden, it makes more of a contribution. It is confusing in garden centres as a lot of Lavender types look the same but if you choose from these three you will have made the best choice for insects.

MOTHERWORT - LATIN NAME - LEONURUS CARDIACA

TYPICAL FLOWERING PERIOD 01/08—1/09

SYMBOLS >>>** POINTS SCORED 58 LARGE PERENNIAL

This is a tall herb up to 1.75 metres, when established, with small flowers but attractive foliage with the appearance of a grey green lions tail. It is recommended by bee keepers to improve the taste of honey but all bees get benefits from it. This is considered invasive in the USA, but not often planted in the UK. A number of factors including our climate, make this a rather more innocent plant when planted in a herb garden in the UK. I did not note invasive tendency myself when cultivating the plant.

WEDDING FLOWER
LATIN NAME—FRANCOA SONCHIFOLIA

TYPICAL FLOWERING PERIOD 20/06—10/08
SYMBOLS >>>>**###**

POINTS SCORED 133 - MEDIUM PERENNIAL
♥ TREE BUMBLEBEE BOMBUS HYPNORUM

One of my favourite plants for sheer diversity of insects that visit. The flowers are orchid like and either white with darker pink markings or in **"Rodgersons Form"** (pictured) rose pink with dark purple markings. Tolerant of some shade but needs a good soil with moisture to do well.

This is buzzing with hoverflies and beetles when in full flower and it is a top tier plant for bees and butterflies.

If the plant is happy the leaves are almost always there even in Winter. Despite its "half hardy" description it has survived over 10 years in my cold clay based garden without complaint. So it can't be that difficult...

STONECROP / ICE PLANT
LATIN NAME - SEDUM/ HYLOTELEPHIUM

TYPICAL FLOWERING PERIOD

10/09—10/10 SYMBOLS >>>###*

POINTS SCORED 78 SMALL PERENNIAL - ROCKERY

The flat flower headed Autumn flowering Stonecrop appears in almost every wildlife gardening book as a plant for insects in particular butterflies. It is if you have a **Small Tortoiseshell** in the area, they will give you much pleasure by visiting.

Some varieties flatter to deceive. The actual period they produce a reward is brief. The unopened developing flower is there for a long time, this is not the flower. For the late Summer plants I have found **Sedum matrona "Telephium"** to be much liked by bees and butterflies and they also like **Sedum "Purple Emperor"** and **"Parish Plum".** Note the new name, this may be found under **Hylotelephium.**

Buy Sedum at a garden centre and look for bees or butterflies actually staying on the flowers, not flying on and off it. Go for **Sedum spectabile** the "unimproved" variety as a number 2 alternative. I would put below this the popular **"Autumn Joy"** which is good for bees, though some of us have had less success with butterflies on this plant.

ABELIA GRANDIFLORA

TYPICAL FLOWERING PERIOD   07/07— 30/10 SYMBOLS >>>>#***

POINTS SCORED   119 Medium Shrub
♥ HONEY BEE APIS MELLIFERA

This is a shrub also available with variegated or plain green leaves. As you will expect, having read this far, (well done!) the basic version is the best, but what a plant this is!

It flowers for four solid months until the frost comes and sometimes beyond, into November. It is very attractive to bees and other insects when they are about. Other than clipping back to shape in Spring it needs little attention and will associate with perennials in a mixed border. Keep it in a sheltered position.

You could also successfully grow this in a large pot, if you have limited room and want to have one good wildlife plant for your patio. I consider this one of the best plants for your wildlife garden.

Above -**Sedum / Hylotelephium Matrona** also known as **Stonecrop or Iceplant**

EVENING PRIMROSE - LATIN NAME-OENOTHERA BIENNIS (ABOVE)

TYPICAL FLOWERING PERIOD 25/06—10/10

SYMBOLS >>### MAX POINTS SCORED 79 MEDIUM SIZED BIENNIAL

Good for moths in the late evening. This plant has a very long flowering period and is best in its "original" form **Oenothera biennis.** It only flowers for one year.

There are other types of Evening Primroses at garden centres. Avoid pink or other shorter varieties that bloom briefly (**Oenothera "Siskiyou Pink"** is in particular woeful) and are of much less usefulness for insects as a result.

They love well drained soil so add some grit. Look for little flat leaved seedlings in Summer, which will flower the following year. Move them when little before the vulnerable tap root develops. The plant is pollinated by moths, butterflies and bees.

Origano "Herrenhausen"

MARJORAM - LATIN NAME - ORIGANUM LAEVIGATUM

TYPICAL FLOWERING PERIOD 05/07—04/09

SYMBOLS >>>>####* MAX POINTS SCORED 126 SMALL PERENNIAL**

Oregano is the same as **Marjoram**. The variety **"Herrenhausen"** is one of the best plants for bees and butterflies of this herb, though not for your kitchen. This has 76% sugar within the nectar, so this concentration of a reward makes the plant popular with all insects. Likes sun and will grow well as border edging. Another good variety is **"Hopleys"**.

Origanum vulgare the native plant of meadows is also attractive to insects but for a shorter flower period and that is a proper edible herb. ♥ Meadow Brown Maniola jurtina butterflies adore the wild plant. Avoid "golden" leaved variety with a shorter flowering period.

THYME - LATIN NAME THYMUS

TYPICAL FLOWERING PERIOD 25/06—20/08

SYMBOLS >>>##* MAX POINTS SCORED 81 SMALL PERENNIAL

Thyme looks like a smaller version of marjoram with its flowers. It likes hot,sunny areas to grow on the edges of paths (but not where you can tread on a bee please!) You can use this as a herb in the kitchen. **Thymus Vulgaris. "Silver Queen"** is a good variety to have. Thymus vulgaris (common thyme) and "Thymus polytrichus subsp. britannicus" attracts many honey bees and bumblebees.

HYSSOP - LATIN NAME AGASTACHE

TYPICAL FLOWERING PERIOD 25/06—20/08

SYMBOLS >>>>##**

**MAX POINTS SCORED; 90
SMALL PERENNIAL**

Hyssop is a herb which is beloved by the bumblebees as in the picture. It is hard to keep away from slugs unfortunately but if you can do that, humanely, you will have an excellent bee plant with this one. "Golden Jubilee" is pictured, which has yellow green leaves and seems the best for insects. Needs well drained soil to perform at its best.

FUSCHIA - LATIN NAME
FUCHSIA MAGELLANICA

TYPICAL FLOWERING PERIOD 05/07 - 10/10

SYMBOLS >>>~~ MAX POINTS SCORED 84

These plants range from half hardy belladonnas to the hedgerow plant of the west of Ireland, **Fuschia magellanica** (pictured) which grows up to 2 metres in height. It is this variety that is excellent for bees and other insects and also flowers until the first frost. The more flamboyant and gaudy fuschias available are (mostly) less likely to get through a frost and offer less to insects. **"Riccatonii"** is a smaller variety which takes up less space. Note that wasps like this plant late in the season.

TOP TIP

Fuschia take a long time to produce its leaves in Spring so take advantage of this by having other cover plants beneath it, such as a small **Geranium** or **Pulmonaria**. They really come into their own in August and September so combine well with **Asters** and **Caryopteris**. Clip back early in the season the twiggy stems if they are too tall as blooms occur on the current year of growth.

Echinacea at Nymans Gardens, Sussex

CONEFLOWER -
LATIN NAME - ECHINACEA PURPUREA

TYPICAL FLOWERING PERIOD 14/07 – 09/09

SYMBOLS >>>#~* POINTS SCORED 64

Echinacea "White Swan" will rarely appear without a bumblebee at a garden centre.

♥ WHITE TAILED BUMBLEBEE BOMBUS LUCORUM

Visits to garden centres proved there was always a free bumblebee with each Echinacea plant. It is fairly easy to grow if you have well drained soil (add grit) and a mostly sunny position. I love **"Magnus"** (dark rose) and **"White Swan"** The plain **Echinacea purpurea** is the easiest to grow. Some of the newer varieties do not seem as attractive to bees and include doubles and oranges, which somehow don't look quite right. Keep it away from slugs and it is a good plant.

FENNEL - LATIN NAME - FOENICULUM VULGARE
FLOWERING PERIOD 01/08 - 10/9   SYMBOLS *~~~ POINTS SCORE 70**

♥ MARMALADE HOVERFLY EPISYRPHUS BALTEATUS

The best plant for hoverflies in late Summer which characteristically hover all around. It is worth growing a good large plant of this. The **"Bronze"** type is better looking than the "Green" for a border . However it does need a warm spot and good soil. Clay soil isn't great for it. But this herb tends to be relatively cheap at garden centres.

Green Fennel, Foeniculum vulgare

SNEEZEWEED - LATIN NAME - HELENIUM AUTUMNALE

TYPICAL FLOWERING PERIOD 25/07—30/08

SYMBOLS >>>*** MAX POINTS SCORED 117 MEDIUM PERENNIAL

They like moist soil in sun, and partly as a result of this and soft new foliage they are very prone to slug damage so need protection from them. At this time of year there are several top bee plants in bloom, the **Abelia**, **Loosestrife** and **Lavender** all doing their bit. Some studies for insects place this above the other plants I mention. **Helenium Autumnale**, which you can buy via mail order from nurseries on the internet is a great insect plant. The variety **"Moerheim Beauty"** (dark orange, top picture) and **Rauchtopas"** (orange and yellow) are also good for solitary bees, as is **"Waldtraut"** and **"The Bishop"** (pictured below).

CULVERS ROOT - LATIN NAME - VERONICASTRUM

TYPICAL FLOWERING PERIOD 24/07—01/08

SYMBOLS >>>>* *# MAX POINTS SCORED 87 LARGE PERENNIAL

One of my favourite plants, but not easy to grow. I look down on fingers that are not green. It LOVES moisture, you have to make a DEEP soil with plenty of nutrients in it otherwise stems will flop. **"Album"** is the toughest plant and very good for bees. **"Fascination"** and **"Lavendelturm"** seem weak on my clay soil, but it probably has not enough sun in my garden. This also has lovely foliage, though you might have to explain to neighbours that you are not growing cannabis as the leaves are superficially similar. Studies have indicated that bees have a preference for the nectar and pollen of this plant, above many others so it is very much worth the effort.

Next door to **Veronicastrum** at the garden centre is the similar named **Veronica** genus, or Speedwell. This has similar spikes of flowers liked by insects but on much smaller plants. I used to grow **Veronica spicata, (45 points)** blue spires loved by bees which is a native wild flower in moist areas of North Europe. Nowadays there are other cultivars such as **"Foxy"** (dark pink) and **"Red Fox".** To me the original plant and **Veronica longifolia** (beautiful blue) are the most durable.

Above - **Veronicastrum Virginicum "Album"**

GLOBE ARTICHOKE LATIN NAME CYNARA SCOLYMUS

TYPICAL FLOWERING PERIOD 01/07 —01/09

SYMBOLS >>># POINTS SCORED 66 LARGE PERENNIAL

The large thistle like luminous flowers of the artichoke are magnets to bumblebees and attract butterflies. The plant likes sunshine, and can grow to 2 metres. It struggles in heavy soil but still blooms. ♥ Red tailed bumblebee Bombus lapidarius pictured below will often be found on these plants.

Lavatera, Inula, Helenium, Crocosmia "Lucifer", Hemerocallis "Frans Hals" and **Ceanothus "Gloire de Versailles"** all join together in July to put on a brilliant show

MONTBRETIA - LATIN NAME - CROCOSMIA

TYPICAL FLOWERING PERIOD 05/07 - 26/07

SYMBOLS >>~~ MAX POINTS SCORED 48 ("LUCIFER" ONLY)

I obtained my plant of **"Lucifer"** from a very old fashioned garden centre, many years ago. I noticed some bees buzzing around it so that sold it to me.

I'm left wondering if my plant is an exception, as most other **Crocosmias** have a limited appeal to bees, but honey bees and wasps love my plant. I am not here to argue with their choice. This may illustrate a local preference for a particular plant as elsewhere I see few insects on this plant.

Easy to grow, the only negative point is a short flowering period, however no other flower makes the impact that this plant does. It is a plant firework.

"Lucifer" Bright red and best for honey bees and the common wasp.

"Harlequin" Hilarious Orange and Yellow combination—later than **"Lucifer."**

"George Davidson" - Orange Yellow.

"Lim Popo" - Orange with red throats.

Avoid— anything labelled as the wild variety. Crocosmia x crocosmiiflora. This is not as special as the above plants. **"Lucifer"** is ok in your wildlife garden, but these and other **Crocosmias** are not special overall for insects.

COMPASS PLANT - LATIN NAME SILPHIUM LACINIATUM

TYPICAL FLOWERING PERIOD 20/7—30/08

SYMBOLS >>>**## MAX POINTS SCORED 98 LARGE PERENNIAL

This has flowers much like **Helianthus "Lemon Queen"** but larger. It is a softer plant, more like a Dahlia. The flowers follow the sun, like a flower clock or compass. It is loved by slugs and if a shoot is damaged by being cut off that shoot will never regrow or flower. It is a beautiful plant best in sun and with a mulch of considerable gravel at its base. Bees and other insects love it. I like to grow it with **Crocosmia "Lucifer"**.

HIMILAYAN HONEYSUCKLE / PHEASANT BUSH

LATIN NAME - LEYCESTERIA FORMOSA

TYPICAL FLOWERING PERIOD 05/07 —10/10

SYMBOLS >>>**- MAX POINTS SCORED 80 LARGE SHRUB

This is really easy to grow. Many more leaves than flowers though. As the season advances, dangling ear rings of purple red berries combine with the small white flowers. Birds such as blackbirds do eat the berries. This is also tolerant of some shade. The only thing you need is room. It is 2 metres plus high and 2 metres across when mature but can be ruthlessly cut back each Spring.

There is also a cultivar called **Leycesteria "Golden Lanterns"** but this offers yellow foliage at the expense of as many flowers, but my **leaf cutter bees** use it to build their nest pods, so I leave this smaller plant, in a corner just for that purpose.

Top Tip

It is possible to make a musical instrument by cutting lengths of the bamboo like stems. An old fashioned activity for kids. You must let the stems dry out completely first (health and safety). Cut so there is the maximum amount of hollow stem to blow into and then cut further to refine a note. The results are a little like the Pan Pipes. If you know what notes are which. And if you don't, have fun finding out by trying out different lengths and widths of shoot!

PURPLE TOADFLAX - LATIN NAME - LINARIA

TYPICAL FLOWERING PERIOD 05/07 - 10/10

SYMBOLS >>>># MAX POINTS SCORED 83 MEDIUM PERENNIAL**

Purple Toadflax (effectively a wild flower which came over from Italy, where it is native) is the best for all types of bees, which love it. It does self seed where happy, but I am usually happy where it self seeds. Other varieties such as **"Canon Went"** (pink) and **"Springside White"** (white, surprisingly) are still fairly good plants for bees and hoverflies but I prefer the intensity of the purple version.

Creeping Toadflax (Linaria repens) rarely found in the wild of Southern England. I am lucky enough to have this in my garden. It likes to grow on or near walls or a dry situation such as gravel. A pretty, medium perennial that fills in difficult gaps with its white and pale blue flowers. In this respect it is good for concentrated planting as it will flower through other flowers. Growers should work with this plant as it is garden worthy and scores a reliable **78 points** in my research. **Honey bees** are the most frequent visitor to this Toadflax.

HEBE - LATIN NAME HEBE

TYPICAL FLOWERING PERIOD 20/06 —20/07 and then 10/09 to 10/10 SYMBOLS >>>>***###

POINTS SCORED 128 MEDIUM OR LARGE SHRUB

♥ BOMBUS LAPIDARIUS RED TAILED BUMBLEBEE (PICTURED)

Hebe "MidSummer Beauty" (pictured left) is my favourite here. Easy to grow, quite large (though can be clipped to a metre square) and comparatively hardy, though the 2018 Winter put my plants back months as the foliage was destroyed. They recovered and did the normal thing of blooming in July and then in September. In fact this plant can flower in January (See the "Season Stretchers Chapter).

The reason some **Hebe** plants are better than others for insects relates to the length of the flowering spike and number of flowers. **Hebe rakaiensis,** a small evergreen shrub rather like box, has flowers that attract all the insects, but only for a few short weeks. Other smaller Hebe have a similar problem.

"Great Orme" which has more pinky flowers than **"MidSummer Beauty"** is smaller, no more than 1.2 metres and is recommended for insects.

Top Tip

Hebe is easy to increase via cuttings. In fact all of my plants were cuttings from a plant from somewhere else. Plants for free! Some plant varieties with thicker fleshy or coloured leaves found at garden centres are not likely to be hardy in the UK to the extent of actually not growing well so are best avoided.

CINQUEFOIL—LATIN NAME POTENTILLA FRUTICOSA "ELIZABETH"

TYPICAL FLOWERING PERIOD 07/07—15/10

SYMBOLS >>>***##~ MAX POINTS SCORED 115 SMALL SHRUB

Potentilla is available in white, pink, yellow, orange and red. There is a massive difference between how long these plants flower, and how good they are for insects. Garden centres will dislike me here but some of these plants currently sold are truly awful. Recommended plants are as follows...

Potentilla fruticosa "Elizabeth" (Buttercup Yellow, above) This is a fabulous plant, long flowering, brilliant for insects, and apparently close to the original wild form, no surprise there. This scores a huge number of points and is well liked by hoverflies and all bees.

"Goldfinger" also yellow, is also a great plant. **"Abbotswood"** is white and one of the more floriferous ones. **"Medicine Wheel"** Yellow flowers early but at the edge of the plant, a peculiar look, but is long flowering.

"Limelight" Yellow centre fades outwards to cream flowers. Buy one at a garden centre in full flower with buds to come but this is mostly a very floriferous plant.

"Pink Beauty" will flower for months.

Not Recommended - unless you want to be perverse to insects, so to speak.

"Red Ace" Dark orange flowers, if you are lucky. **"Tangerine" "Red Robin AKA Marian"** Can be shy to flower. In my case, maybe not at all, ever.

The above are shrubs. Confusingly there are also perennials **(Silverweed)** with attractive serrated leaves referred to as Potentilla such as **"Gibsons Scarlet"** these are poor in comparison to the better plants above Don't buy these by mistake!

LOOSESTRIFE LYTHRUM SALICARIA

TYPICAL FLOWERING PERIOD 07/07—30/09

SYMBOLS >>>>*#### MAX POINTS SCORED 121 MEDIUM PERENNIAL**

It is sad to read about how plants can be introduced into another country and become invasive to the extent they affect the natural balance, making it illegal to plant them. This is the case with **Loosestrife** which was introduced to the USA in the 1800's and sadly now runs rampant.

In the UK, the wild plant is a bully in waterside situations and loves saturated places. There are also however types that are suitable for gardens and these are non invasive. For insects these are fantastic plants and indeed **Loosestrife** is one of the top plants for bees and butterflies. The problems with the native plant come from seeds (2 million on each plant!) which will germinate if you have boggy soil. The key to control is to cut the flower stems down before they can set seed.

A list of well behaved (and not naughty at all) **Loosestrife** plants

Lythrum salicaria "Rosy Gem" Pictured above, this is the plant I grow and I never found it invasive. **"Robert"** is also good and a rich rosy purple. **"Swirl"** a slightly smaller variety with clouds of flowers more widely spaced than other types. This one just stays where it is and does not spread at all. **"The Rocket"** has a good flowering period whereas **"Blush"** has a slightly shorter flowering period than the others. If you like a washed out pink, this is fantastic!!

I'm not stopping you growing the UK native in your UK garden, but if you have a boggy garden I would advise against it. PLEASE note the comments made above if you are reading in the USA you should not plant it, or any cultivars, there.

MICHAELMAS DAISY - LATIN NAME - WAS ASTER NOW SYMPHYOTRICHUM

TYPICAL FLOWERING PERIOD "MöNCH" 25/07 —20/9

SYMBOLS "MöNCH >>>*### POINTS SCORED 109 MEDIUM PERENNIAL**

Aster frikartii "Mönch" is known as a Michaelmas daisy however it starts blooming by early August and finishes in October which is more than twice as long as the others. In a large clump its simple flowers are good for bees, butterflies and hoverflies. It is late (like all Asters) to show itself in Spring so mark its placing carefully to avoid treading on it. This plant likes a mostly sunny position for success.

Don't be tempted by other **"Frikartii"** types as they are lovely plants but not as good as **"Mönch"** which I like for the long flowering period.

The traditional Michaelmas daisies flower around Michaelmas day which is 29th September. This is getting to the time when the numbers of insects start to deplete so these make a valuable contribution before Winter sets in. Weather conditions at the time have an impact. So some years these daisies will be covered in insects on the newly emerged flowers and other years not. It is a gamble, what will turn up? These are the ones that I recommend for a wildlife garden and they score a maximum of **65 points** in my study.

Aster "Little Pink Beauty" This is very good for bees and reasonably early. It is short, below 30 cms in height.

Aster "Little Carlow" I understand on good authority this is very good for bees though it is too similar to "Mönch" if growing together, you need a contrast.

Aster nova belgii "Crimson Brocade" Rose and yellow centred flowers. Tall, sometimes late but beautiful flowers. **"Crimson Beauty"** is similar.

Aster "Winston Churchill" A late one this, I try and give it a sunnier position to encourage it out earlier, blue purple single flowers on stout, tall shoots about 100cm in height but flowers for nearly a month unless there is an early frost.

"Andenkan an Alma Pötschke" I have grown this plant for years, it is a mid September appearance with its rosy flowers, though only for a few short weeks.

Avoid **"Bahamas"** short in both stature and flowering period. If you want a short one, try **"Jenny"** a beautiful purple rose flower on short stems and **"White Ladies"** another "Nova Belgii" variety in white. For small flowers try **"Divaricatus"**

Asters may suffer with mildew, but don't spray them with chemicals. The varieties mentioned are LESS likely to suffer. You should be looking for a New England or "Nova Angliae" type.

Note that *Symphyotrichum is the new name for Aster though garden centres still refer to Aster, as this is a hugely confusing change. I say it has to be ASTER...! We have been calling them this name for over a century, so why change it?*

Above **Aster Crimson Beauty** makes a dramatic show in early October.

Below **Aster frikatii Mönch** growing around **Pittosporum "Irene Patterson"**

COMMON (PERFOLIATE) ST JOHNS WORT - HYPERICUM PERFORATUM

A small Summer yellow wild flower which appears naturally in my garden and may appear in yours. It only produces pollen, but is loved by bees, it will fit in almost anywhere, you can obtain it from wildlife nurseries or from seed. This scores 40 points (Key >>*) **Related Plants** Avoid the large bush **Hypericum "Hidcote"** as insects rarely trouble it. The short flowering ground cover plant **Hypericum calycinum (Rose of Sharon)** is too invasive for most gardens. The berried variety **Hypericum elatum "Elstead"** is however, briefly, very good for bees and works well as it will be tolerant of a shady corner that does not get sunshine for most of the day.

CALIFORNIAN LILAC LATIN NAME CEANOTHUS "GLOIRE DE VERSAILLES"

TYPICAL FLOWERING PERIOD 01/07 —20/09

SYMBOLS >>>*~ POINTS SCORED 90 LARGE SHRUB**

A glorious tall shrub. Hoverflies and bees love it. It might not always be hardy but mine grows well in an unpromising position. It flowers on the last years growth, so be careful with pruning of the plant. It gets to 2 metres and has a lovely fragrance that carries over a large area. It also flowers randomly nearer Christmas time in many gardens with its light blue cluster of flowers. There is a weak pink version which I have never seen to grow that well. Again it is common for bred colour varieties to not be as good as the original plant. Stick with the tried and tested with this and other plants!

SHASTA DAISIES - LATIN NAME - LEUCANTHEMUM

TYPICAL FLOWERING PERIOD 12/07 —10/09

SYMBOLS ># MAX POINTS SCORED 54 MEDIUM PERENNIAL**

There are a number of these white daisies in this book, starting with the **Ox Eye daisies** in May and finishing with the **Hungarian Daisy** in September and October. The original Shasta Daisy **(Leucanthemum superbum)** was bred in 1890 and my mum grew this for many years. I have the original plant in my garden too. The advantages are that it repeat flowers, is more tolerant of Winter wet conditions, and shade. It has a slightly ragged charm as it needs staking in case it decides to flop. The proliferation of other plants is such that you could be tempted by one of the many types that just flower once and call it a day. Of those available I like **"Alaska"** which is similar to the main Shasta Daisy. **"Snowcap"** is an earlier flowering much smaller plant but not especially repeat flowering with me. I avoid **"Broadway Lights"** due to its intolerance of my clay conditions and double flowers such as **"Wirral Supreme"** that have less of the central disc for insects and provide hardly if any sustenance for them.

TOP TIP

Stake **Shasta Daisies** with twiggy supports in early Spring which will stop them flopping when they get taller (as they did in my garden) pictured above.

CHICORY - LATIN NAME - CICHORIUM

TYPICAL FLOWERING PERIOD 01/07 — 01/08 >>> 58 points**

With untidy foliage, like a weed, and an untidy habit, one would wonder, "why bother?" The beautiful light blue flowers, which close as the day goes on, are very attractive to bees. The ungainly aspect of the plant can be helped by staking. It also takes up little room if you do this, and is a great plant for a corner that gets a few hours of sun a day. It is a tough perennial that will return for you next year. Let plants in front of it cover up its weedy looking base foliage if tidiness does matter.

TEASEL - LATIN NAME - DIPSACUS -TYPICAL FLOWERING PERIOD 10/07 - 30/08 SYMBOLS >>>## POINTS SCORED 73 LARGE BIENNIAL 2 METRES**

English native and a biennial. It is tall, quite stately actually and looks like a large, pinkish thistle. Bumblebees love this plant and insects drink water from the small wells formed between its prickly leaves. It isn't one for a tidy border though it tends to look good enough where it appears elsewhere.

The only problem is that it might appear too much as it will self seed everywhere. A wild, wildflower and whilst not outlawed in the UK, it cannot be planted in many countries including the USA. Seed heads attract goldfinches but don't leave too many unless you want a Teasel garden.

SPIRAEA LATIN NAME SPIRAEA JAPONICA "ANTHONY WATERER"

TYPICAL FLOWERING PERIOD 01/07 - 20/08

SYMBOLS >>## POINTS SCORED 73 MEDIUM SHRUB**

Spiraea are small shrubs often planted by the local Council in car parks. The most common yellow leaved variety **"Gold Mound"** has flowers of pink and is of some interest to pollinating insects though not so easy on the eye. It is **Spiraea "Anthony Waterer"** with its deep rose flowers that wins most insect visitors. It has a reasonable flowering period and can be cut back after flowering. There is also an unusual variety **"Genpei"** which has part pink part white flowers and **"Magic Carpet"** will also attract insects.

Avoid **Spiraea "Steeple Bush"** the candyfloss fluffy type flowers are brief, and it is relatively unattractive. Avoid **"Pink Ice"** a lovely foliage plant but with very few flowers. Many other types are visited less by insects

MEXICAN SUNFLOWER - TITHONIA ROTUNDIFOLIA "TORCH"

TYPICAL FLOWERING PERIOD 25/07 - 02/09

SYMBOLS >>**## 70 POINTS SCORED - LARGE ANNUAL

Like all Sunflowers, this attracts a wide range of insects. It is an option to grow in a large pot in a sheltered position where it will attract bees and hoverflies and if they are about, butterflies as well. It has voluptuous foliage that takes up a lot of space!

YARROW - LATIN NAME ACHILLEA MILLEFOLIUM

TYPICAL FLOWERING PERIOD 10/07 - 20/09

SYMBOLS >>***## 88 POINTS SCORED SMALL / MEDIUM PERENNIAL

The native wild yarrow is a flat topped, small, white flower of grassland and meadows and this is a clue to the open sunny conditions favoured by the cultivated varieties of the plant which come in many colours. They are all attractive for hoverflies and for butterflies, such as ❤ Pyronia tithonus, the Gatekeeper so plants selected here score best with a longer flowering period.

92

"Cloth of Gold" is pictured above and often grown as a reliable plant up to 1.5 metres tall. **"Coronation Gold"** is similar, to 1 metre I grow **"Terracotta"** an unusual shade (picture below) mid yellow and orange which is about the same height. **"Moonshine"** is lemon yellow and shorter 0.5 of a metre **"Cerise Queen"** (pictured below) can be a bit vigorous but is easily controlled. **"Red Velvet"** has flowers that retain colour for a long time. Avoid **"The Pearl",** an Achillea with rather different looking puffs of flowers and not really for the insects.

TOP TIP

Cut Achillea right back to a few centimetres after flowering, keeping them well watered at this point, and you will most likely see more flowers a month later.

Achillea Cerise Queen (Above) **Terracotta** (Below)

GLOBE THISTLE LATIN NAME ECHINOPS

TYPICAL FLOWERING PERIOD 05/07 —10/08

SYMBOLS >>>## POINTS SCORED 80 MEDIUM PERENNIAL**

The globe thistle (pictured above) has round purple, blue or white flowers, all of which are very attractive to the bumblebees. It works best in a wild garden as the foliage can be a bit coarse. It needs a position with direct sun each day but will grow successfully in a slightly shady place. The globes stay on the plant after flowering and look good in Winter. Pick "Taplow Blue" (pictured above) and "Arctic Glow" (White).

SEA HOLLY LATIN NAME ERYNGIUM—SEA HOLLY

TYPICAL FLOWERING PERIOD 01/7 —10/08

SYMBOLS >>>>##*POINTS SCORED 98 SMALL PERENNIAL**

Varieties **"Alpinum"** and "**Bourgatii**" are great, as is **"Tripartitum"**. These are drought resistant when established as garden plants, grow in gravel or well drained soil in the sunshine. This is like a very small version of **Echinops,** but the blue of the flower is more intense and the interest of insects can be quite intense as well! For a silvery aluminium type flower, go for the Biennial **"Miss Wilmotts Ghost"**, unusual , but as good as the blue Sea Holly for bees.

DENDRANTHEMA WEYRICHII TYPICAL FLOWERING PERIOD 25/07 - 18//08

SYMBOLS >>>   POINTS SCORED 58 SMALL ROCKERY PLANT**

This pinkish white daisy needs sharp drainage and full sun. This is a small alpine plant no more than a few centimetres tall, for a small space and you could grow it successfully in a small pot. It is good for bees and hoverflies.

BLAZING STAR LATIN NAME - LIATRIS SPICATA

TYPICAL FLOWERING PERIOD 20/07 - 02/09

SYMBOLS >>>>## POINTS SCORED 91 MEDIUM PERENNIAL**

Writing this book means that sometimes I have to acknowledge a plant that I would not favour myself, but which insects actually love.

Such it is with **Liatris,** which flowers from the top of the stem downwards, a habit which in my eyes at least makes it look a bit odd when the top is dead and the bottom is in bloom. It's a mind thing, like a purple tomato. But the foliage is very attractive, especially beside water and in reality, what do my opinions matter? Is it more important to have a good plant for insects than aesthetics? They have voted on this one… Bees butterflies and hoverflies love it. It is a fantastic plant for them.

This needs a sunny site, will fail in shade and slugs and mice like the shoots and roots. This makes growing it potentially frustrating. I grow **Loosestrife** that looks a little similar, but never entertains a slug or a mouse. **Liatris spicata "Kobold"** pictured above is better looking than the white version **"Alba"** that has the white dead brown combination on the flower stems, the same as white **Buddleia davidii.** Insects don't really mind, they won't judge aesthetics!

TICKSEED - LATIN NAME - COREOPSIS VERTICILLATA

TYPICAL FLOWERING PERIOD 01/07 - 01/10

SYMBOLS >>>>*## POINTS SCORED 103 SMALL PERENNIAL**

This is a mid season plant that has brightly coloured beautiful daisies for hoverflies and bees, so I keep trying despite the tendency for slugs to eat the leaves. Many varieties are available such as **"Moonbeam"** (Pale Lemon) **"Flying Saucers"** (what a name—bright yellow) **"Sunfire"** (yellow and red) and the tall **Coreopsis gigantea ("Mayfield Giant")** are all super for insects. **Coreopsis tripteris** can top 2 metres. The others are small plants which I like growing in a pot, in the sunshine. It dislikes Winter wet. This is one of the best Summer plants for hoverflies in my study.

Helianthus "Lemon Queen"—pictured near Merano, Italy, 2nd September

PERENNIAL SUNFLOWER LATIN NAME HELIANTHUS "LEMON QUEEN"

TYPICAL FLOWERING PERIOD 20/07 —25/10 SYMBOLS >>>>###***

POINTS SCORED 124 LARGE PERENNIAL - UP TO 2 METRES

💜 COMMON CARDER BEE BOMBUS PASCUORUM

The perennial sunflower is easy to grow in the sunshine, in good soil, that does not dry out. You can't negotiate with this plant and offer it anything less as you need the best results. The trick is to get this into bloom as early as possible. Small shoots and petals around the flowers can be attacked by slugs and snails but the vigour of the plant wins out. This plant will then flower until the first frosts and is a good indicator of overall bee activity late in the season as it is a preference plant above most others. The flowers are not as large as the annual Sunflower, but on a good plant you will get many of them before the season closes.

In Italy I saw the plant covered in bees including continental species which also love the plant. Its easy to collect pollen and nectar from any sunflower, so it understandably scores well in my research.

Allow room for a good clump, it will repay you. As the quality of plants from growers does vary it makes sense to buy at a garden centre, look for a group of buds at the top of the stem with successor buds to follow.

There are other Helianthus at the garden centre sometimes. *Avoid the* **Willow leaved Sunflower (Helianthus salicifolius)** as this is grown for its foliage and not for its tiny and sparing flowers. **Helianthus multiflorus** has a beautiful variety known as **"Capenoch Star"** which has a shorter flowering period, larger flowers, but is harder to keep going than Lemon Queen.

Above - **Caryopteris clandonensis "Worcester Gold"** Pictured 10th September.

BLUEBEARD - LATIN NAME - CARYOPTERIS INCANA / CLANDONENSIS

TYPICAL FLOWERING PERIOD 01/09—15/10 / 23/08 —20/09

SYMBOLS >>>>##** POINTS SCORED 121 / 117

This was the plant that gave me the idea for this book.

Seeing this plant in a West Country garden at 7pm on an early September evening, literally covered with insects and other flowering plants in the same garden abandoned, made me realise the immense difference our choice as gardeners can make, to how supportive our gardens are of insects and other wildlife.

This remains one of the best bee plants for later in the season though it has no capacity to go beyond its allotted flowering period. It will flower earlier or later, for around a month depending on plant type, situation and preceding Summer.

There is a range of different plants with slightly different outcomes, described over the page, and one or two worth avoiding…

TOP TIP

Cut back the plant in May to about 15 centimetres off the ground overall and take cuttings with these shoots. By Autumn these will be big enough to pot up, and keep in a sheltered place in case of Winter losses, something that can happen with **Caryopteris** as a combination of cold and wet finishes them off.

These potted up plants can usefully fill gaps by other earlier flowering plants, as **Caryopteris** does not get going until later in the season with its leaves and growth.

CHOICES FOR CARYOPTERIS

"Caryopteris incana" isn't reliably hardy so needs a sunny all day position with gritty soil but it is liked very much by bees. The blue is lighter and most beautiful. Varieties include **"Kew Blue"** & **"Sunshine Blue"** (with yellow foliage). These tend to be later into bloom, late September early October.

Caryopteris clandonensis varieties are more hardy and of a deeper shade of blue.

"Heavenly Blue" is often seen and is a good dark blue variety flowering a little later as does **"Dark Knight"** a variety that is often available.

"Worcester Gold" flowers August to September (with yellow emerging foliage). It does flower well for a "sport" or foliage variety but needs perfect conditions to do so, they will not cooperate if slightly shaded.

"Summer Sorbet" has some of the quality of **"Worcester Gold"** but is not as good.

"Stephi" A chance pink grey flowering seedling. I remain a fan of the blue plants, known as "bluebeard" and not of what is effectively "pinkbeard"! Ditto for versions such as "Pink Perfection" for example.

CONEFLOWER - LATIN NAME RUDBECKIA

TYPICAL FLOWERING PERIOD
20/07 —15/10

POINTS SCORED - SEE COMMENTS BELOW

Out of all the plants recommended for bees, **Rudbeckia** was overall the most disappointing in my study. In particular **"Goldsturm"** which is found at EVERY garden centre. Is **"Goldsturm"** a dud for bees? I have found it so!

I have resolved to continue to grow it until I see something, but this plant is abandoned in favour of **Caryopteris** or **Helianthus** so at the very least it is a low preference plant for insects as a whole.

Pictured is **Rudbeckia "Summerina Brown"** a brand new variety that at least has something for the bees as they are attracted to it. This though, needs well drained soil and responds best to full sun to succeed.

BLANKET FLOWER - LATIN NAME GAILLARDIA

TYPICAL FLOWERING PERIOD 25/07 - 10/9 SYMBOLS >>>**

POINTS SCORED 62 ♥ WHITE TAILED BUMBLEBEE BOMBUS LUCORUM

A very cheerful mid late Summer flower, this is very much liked by bumblebees.

The plant **"Goblin"** is often sold (and pictured) though remember this is rather short, not more than 20 centimetres high, so suited for the front of a sunny border.

"Burgundy" and **"Celebration"** are other good varieties to go for. This perennial may not be long lived before it needs replacing.

HOREHOUND BLACK/WHITE

LATIN NAME - BALLOTA

TYPICAL FLOWERING PERIOD 10/07 —20/08 SYMBOLS >>>**

POINTS SCORED 68/73

Black Horehound **(Ballota nigra)** has small purple flowers with silver foliage and is somewhat nettle like in appearance. They are visited by hoverflies and bees including rarer solitary bees.

They like well drained soil and sunshine but are fully hardy.

Marrubium Vulgare, also known as White Horehound has the appearance of a more woolly, silver leaved mint. In a sunny position this is a great bee plant.

HEDGE WOUNDWORT

LATIN NAME - STACHYS SYLVATICA - NATIVE

TYPICAL FLOWERING PERIOD 10/07 —30/08 SYMBOLS >>>#** 63 POINTS

A hedgerow plant that often visits gardens, this is a great plant for solitary bees and other smaller insects. It looks slightly like a flowering nettle, is generally unassuming but worth including in a wild corner. It is tolerant of some shade. In addition it is a food plant of the **Garden Tiger** and **Small Rivulet Moth.**

Gaillardia in all its gaudy glory, 30th July

Avoid double blooms such as on the far left for **Dahlias.** Some semi-double plants are still great for bees, if they have an open centre (centre picture) but the best choices for insects are fully single flowers, as on the far right.

DAHLIA LATIN NAME DAHLIA

TYPICAL FLOWERING PERIOD 02/07 —10/10

SYMBOLS >>>*# POINTS SCORED 95 SMALL MEDIUM PERENNIAL**

Dahlias come towards the end of the season with a huge variety of colours and shapes. So which ones are best for insects?

A general principle for buying wildlife friendly plants is that single flowers are the best though some semi double dahlia plants are ok. Double flowers like the one above left, attract nothing and for the purpose of this book should be avoided! Unfortunately the majority of available Dahlias are fully double, so look for the types mentioned on the opposite page.

The flowers of single types are loved by all bees and hoverflies and can provide a last supper before Winter for many insects. They can be tricky to grow in a cold garden.

Planting Advice. Dahlias grow from tubers (a bit like a potato) and are not normally hardy. They need taking up at the first frost and to be stored in a frost free, dry, place. Then in Spring after the last frost put in pots of well drained soil and keep watering them at this point. On placing outdoors, this plant is very susceptible to slug damage, they love the soft leaves. A straw poll of my friends shows that many people buy dahlias only to find they disappear a week later for an apparently mysterious reason!! To avoid this I tend to grow in pots and keep in the middle of a patio to try and avoid slug temptation as slugs don't like crossing a dry patio.

Recommended - The "Bishop" Series (Up to 1.5 metres)

Dahlia "Bishop of Llandaff" Dark red foliage and bright red flowers. Tall and relatively easy in a sunny spot perhaps on the edge of a wall or other warm area such as a path. This can get tall, up to 1.5 metres. If you want a less intense colour, try **"Bishop of Auckland"** (picture opposite, right) which is a darker red.

"Bishop of Leicester" Pink with a darker pink / red centre.

"Bishop of York" Charming lemon yellow.

"Bishop of Oxford" Fantastic orange.

The tall "Bishop" types are well established, long cultivated plants.

"Moonfire" Light orange with darker orange centre up to 1 metre.

"Waltzing Matilda" Pink peach with touches of red, an open single flower to 75 cm.

Twynings "After Eight White" Single, distinguished but not over tall, a bit like the writer of this book. This plant has dark, contrasting,foliage.

Twynings "Smartie" Purple White bi-colour is an incredible flower but difficult.

"Brantwood" Intense rose purple.

"Bee Happy" is a "collarette" dahlia with a few minor frills and ruffles. It has a dark pink centre and a light pink outer edge 60 –90 centimetres tall. The flowers are smaller but the centre disc of pollen and nectar is larger. **"Night Butterfly"** is special, if you want something very select and exotic. This is dark red with white to pink contrasting ruffles, in a beautiful intricate pattern, but still good for bees.

"Fascination" (pictured opposite centre) is about as far towards as double flower as you can go with dahlias. Bees love the flower, and the intense shade of pink will be loved by some humans too.

HUNGARIAN DAISY- LATIN NAME - LEUCANTHEMELLA SEROTINA

TYPICAL FLOWERING PERIOD 10/09 - 10/10

SYMBOLS >>> POINTS SCORED 56 MEDIUM PERENNIAL**

We are getting towards the full stop of the gardening year, and one of the last punctuation points is this plant. It is a beautiful daisy, like a white sunflower, or a larger version of our native **Ox-Eye Daisy**. It likes moisture retentive soil, and won't help you if it dries out. If bees or hoverflies or even butterflies are about from the 2nd week of September when it starts to flower, they will turn up to say hello. But it only really gets going in the first week of October.

It is a gamble but this tall and elegant plant is worthwhile. This might flower earlier if we do have a warmer Autumn climate in years to come.

BUGBANE or BLACK COHOSH

LATIN NAME ACTAEA or CIMICIFUGA

TYPICAL FLOWERING PERIOD 20/08 —10/10

SYMBOLS >>>##**

POINTS SCORED 83

Can have an unpleasant smell and not always easy to grow but beloved of bees (and late butterflies) when in full bloom. This large perennial needs partial shade and a good soil with plenty of nutrients which retains moisture for a couple of years after planting, it can deal with dry shade after that time.

CLIMBING HYDRANGEA— LATIN NAME PILEOSTEGIA VIBURNOIDES

TYPICAL FLOWERING PERIOD 15/08 —06/10

SYMBOLS >>>>** SCORE 73 POINTS LARGE CLIMBER (2 METRES PLUS)

Fantastic Bee plant - self clinging climber. Flowers are white clouds. Plant beneath a fairly sunny wall and wait for the slow progress to get to 2 metres. It may take 5 years to establish and produce the panicles of flowers, seen above. The plant is hardy and the reward for insects is definitely worth it for them!

PURPLE TOP LATIN NAME VERBENA BONARIENSIS

TYPICAL FLOWERING PERIOD 15/07 —20/10

SYMBOLS >>>>*#### POINTS SCORED 144 MEDIUM PERENNIAL**

♥ CARDER BEE BOMBUS PASCUORUM

For small spaces this is a brilliant plant, takes up little width but offers broad purple panicles of flowers a metre or more tall for several months that are loved by bees, butterflies (a favourite plant) and hoverflies. Goldfinches visit in Winter to eat the seeds. So don't cut the plant back in Autumn.

Carder Bee above on Verbena

This grows well through other plants such as **Helianthemum** and is easy in a sunny sheltered position.

For me, when this plant ceases flowering at the first frost of the season this plant represents the end of the gardening year. It is also the end of these chapters on flowering plants though there are more selections through this book in the chapter on Trees, the chapter on Ponds and the chapter on Concentrated Ecology Planting.

If you take all these plants together, there is a terrific variety of different choices for a garden. So my argument is, why do we have to plant anything else that is NOT good for wildlife?

The proportion of wildlife *beneficial* plants in our gardens, council planting and public spaces is currently very low from my own observations. Imagine the huge difference planting only these plants could make. This book becomes an initiative with a huge amount of potential to improve biodiversity.

And that is my final message from this chapter, it is one of hope. We can all really make a difference, even in a small space, by selecting the best plants for wildlife and for insects.

CHAPTER 6 —SEASON STRETCHERS

Every year is different. Sometimes I have many insects in the garden come October. This year there were many bees, the year before, very few. With climate getting warmer, we will see longer forage seasons for some insects and it is important for plants to be out flowering for them.

Whatever causes climate change isn't something we need to debate here.

But climate change exists and is one more danger (to add to all the others) to bees and other pollinating insects. This was clear in 2018, when April, June and July had no rain at all over a large section of the UK. Parched ground is not helpful to butterflies who have a finite life of 20—30 days looking to lay eggs for the next year with potentially nothing for caterpillars to feed on. Population decimation is possible in these circumstances. Bumblebees suffered a population drop in some areas which had a knock on impact on the population in 2019. These insects have evolved over millions of years to follow the (usually dampish) UK weather trends and cannot instantly adapt to dramatic changes in the climate. Bees nesting on the ground are vulnerable to extreme weather events, such as flooding.

Imagine, in a very mild Winter, how a yearly cycle is disrupted by no reset button, no period of cold weather or proper Winter. Confusion reigns within a bee colony that does not know which season it is in! Who can blame them for being confused?

This chapter looks at what we can do by placing a focus on plants that will bloom towards the end of the season, and even during the Winter. Such plants will be of use to bees that emerge in unseasonal mild weather.

Weather is of course such an important factor on whether an early bee emerges to feed. Below 8 Celsius or 48 Fahrenheit a honey bee is unlikely to fly though bumblebees with their fur coats do manage to emerge at lower temperatures. Bees do not have protection from cold and rain, so it has to be dry, and sunny, and warm enough.

Plants such as **Hazel** (which blooms January to February on average) would attract bees and other insects if the weather was not so cold. In fact bees can go crazy for Hazel in a warmer climate. Many early plants such as cultivated Tulips or Daffodils have nothing much to offer. **Aconites and Snowdrops** are better for early bees in February with the best early plants being **Heather** and **Crocus.**

Early in the year there are few other insects about, but feeding emerging bees which are (mostly) on the wing from February to March, is of vital importance. Some early hoverflies do appear in February. There is a variation of as much as a month between when the early plants appear, dependant on how mild or cold the previous period was.

However it is actually warmer Winters which can be most problematic. On warm Winter days honey bees will fly, and without available forage they use up their honey stores too quickly and starve (if allowed to emerge from the hives). Active bumblebee queens will also die, as they use up their "fat" reserves. So we need to have plants that will provide forage at this time but we should also expect that they may not be visited every year.

CHRISTMAS ROSE LATIN NAME—HELLEBORE

TYPICAL FLOWERING PERIOD DECEMBER—APRIL

SYMBOLS >>~ SCORE 57

♥ BUFF TAILED BUMBLEBEE – BOMBUS TERRESTRIS (PICTURE 27/10)

These plants are often in flower at Garden Centres as early as October.

However in my garden they don't get going until the **Crocus** has made its appearance. Such is the business of Garden Centres where flowering period may be somewhat earlier than the reality you discover the next year!

From my research, the white plants are most attractive to bees including varieties of **Helleborus hybridus** and **Helleborus niger.** If you plant them, don't move them. Place in a shady position where they do not get too much Winter wet. But be warned, these are expensive plants (£12 or more each) and they might not come back the year after they are planted if they just don't like where they are. Never shift them!

They do provide nectar for bees but the actual number of likely days they will be visited is few. One option is to plant in a large pot, in a sunny position, and hope they will visit on one of those rare Winter days. In that context this is a great "season stretcher."

Another related plant is the **"Stinking Hellebore"** **Helleborus foetidus**. This blooms later and is a (rare) native of the British Isles. It is attractive, when conditions are right, to early bees and is easy to grow.

Chimonanthus praecox or "Winter Sweet" is often recommended for bees in Winter and will attract them with its fragrance in suitable weather conditions.

Mahonia x media Charity

The bright yellow, upright flowers are produced in open spikes during early to mid Winter. Flowers... sprays of blue fruits covered with a white... Height and Spread in 10 years:... 4m × 1.8m (10ft × 5ft 6in). Position:... Will grow well in any soil... Planting:... Soak the root ball... flower at... Variety of... time...

Lonicera purpusii "Winter Beauty" is also a fragrant plant and a climber that only blooms in January, but this can bring the buff tails to your garden.

There are several very attractive and fragrant varieties of **Mahonia** which flower in the dead of Winter – as opposed to early Spring – which do the trick of providing emergency supplies very nicely, and will sit comfortably in a slightly shadier spot. They have healthy looking, stiff, glossy foliage when not in flower, and their berries are good for the birds. **Mahonia x media 'Charity'** is one of my favourites (Pictured left). It does grow to 2 metres.

Many plants that qualify as "Season Stretchers" offer flowers at the end of the season, in that unpredictable time between cooler wetter weather and the first frosts. This is perhaps the most important period, as this could get longer if the climate gets milder due to climate change.

These are plants that in a reliable way, bloom until the first frosts or "out of season". A perfect example of this is **Hebe "MidSummer Beauty"**. The picture below shows it blooming in January though more normally my plants bloom again in

September or October, Though no bees visited in January this year, the flowers would be great bee forage if they did.

The following "Season Stretchers" have detailed entries in other chapters.

Single flowered Marigolds (Calendula) will bloom until, and sometimes beyond, the first frost.

Ceanothus "Gloire De Versailles" frequently flowers beyond September and has on occasion flowered in November. This is a very useful plant for a variety of insects in Summer, so would be visited out of season in warm weather by pretty much anything that is about.

Abelia grandiflora— Can flower until November slightly beyond any light frosts.

Fuchsia magellanica blooms until the first frosts.

Helianthus "Lemon Queen" doesn't always get to late October, but can get to November if there is sunny mild weather. The best late flowering perennial for insects.

Aster frickarti "Mönch" flowers until the first frosts, as does the annual **"Cosmos"** if deadheaded on a regular basis.

Leucanthemella serotina, as one of the closing points of supply for early Autumn insects is blooming for the only time in the year and usually up to the first frosts.

Aralia elata "Variegata" flowers very late and is one of the top sources for late bees, (though it has some negative features ie thorns!). The Strawberry Tree, **Arbutus unedo is** well visited by the bees between September and October and is a 6 metre high tree with evergreen foliage.

Lavatera shrubs can also bloom up to October, especially if they have been vigorous enough during the season to need to be cut back.

Oenothera the evening primrose is by nature a biennial. So it will most naturally want to flower as long as possible and the odd bloom often comes out even slightly beyond the first light frost.

Penstemon "Garnet" will often have flowering shoots right up to the final knockings in November, though you will have to clip back half of the plant in June to make this happen reliably.

Potentilla "Elizabeth" just keeps blooming until frost forces it to stop, as does **Verbena bonariensis.**

Caryopteris have several varieties some of which do bloom late, into October but no capacity to repeat flower once done.

Ivy, Hedera helix is a valuable late source of pollen and native plant though I would not especially recommend it being planted in a small garden. Variegated or cultivated versions in Garden Centres offer nothing, other than shelter, for insects.

CHAPTER 7 - INSECTS, THE BIRDS AND THE TREES

This book is focused towards insects, but this chapter has several purposes in that it looks at...

The problems trees are facing and the possible impact to insect population.

What trees or very large shrubs are favoured by insects at all stages of the life cycle.

The importance of insects to birds and which trees are recommended for gardens.

TREES ARE FACING ILLNESS

Everything in our environment is facing some kind of peril, and trees are no exception. In the 1970's we lost almost all of our Dutch Elms from our UK countryside. That was a loss of 60 million trees since the original 1920 outbreak, All the insects that exclusively fed, or relied on the ecosystem of Dutch Elms, vanished too. So let us have a look at the current problems our trees are facing and the possible impact. The information is from various sources but mostly from the Forestry Commission.

SUDDEN OAK DEATH SYNDROME

A misleading title for a devastating disease for American Oaks. So far the UK population of oak trees is holding up against this invader though this cannot be relied upon going forward. However this disease has been mostly fatal when found on Larch trees. It can also infect Southern Beech, Red Oak, Holm Oak and, increasingly, Sweet Chestnut.

Larch is a commercially important forestry species in the UK and if this was to spread, it will have a major effect on the forestry industry.

RESULT
WILL KILL MOST LARCH TREES IT INFECTS AND MAKE OTHERS SICK

ACUTE OAK DECLINE

This is a disease which is now affecting many thousands of trees in England from East Anglia to the Midlands up to the Welsh Border and then down towards the South Coast. It affects Sessile and English Oak Trees. This is an unexplained infection of bacterial origin which may be spread by the oak jewel beetle. It is a serious threat to the most important tree we have ecologically for insects and birds.

RESULT
WILL KILL MOST OAK TREES IT INFECTS WITHIN 5 YEARS OF INFECTION

CHALARA—ASH DIEBACK

This disease was confirmed in the UK in 2012. It is an infection of fungal origin. The tree will be killed after a period of up to 10 years or sometimes more after a period of gradual then less gradual, decline.

In areas such as the Peak District the principle tree is the Ash, the death of 9 out of 10 Ash trees (as happened in Denmark) is going to alter the characteristics of these beautiful areas, and elsewhere, forever. There are 90 million Ash trees in the UK

RESULT
FATAL IN 90—95% OF CASES. THIS IS A BIGGER DANGER TO OUR NATIVE TREES THAN DUTCH ELM DISEASE OF THE 1970'S

SWEET CHESTNUT BLIGHT

This killed an estimated 3.5 Billion Trees in the USA in the first half of the century. This fungal infection may be less severe in Europe than it was in the USA but is still, usually, fatal to the trees it affects. A recent outbreak in 2017 in Reading , Derbyshire and Essex may or may not now be contained but new outbreaks of the disease were found during 2019 in London, West Sussex and Cornwall according to forestresearch.gov

RESULT
A DISASTER FOR TREES IF THIS FUNGUS WERE TO SPREAD AGAIN

PINE NEEDLE BLIGHT

Another fungus, this leads to conifers such as Scots Pine and Corsican Pine gradually losing their needles, and they then become defoliated.

Sadly, 70% of Corsican Pines have this disease and Scots Pine may be vulnerable also. Not all plants will die but some will, and others will have an appearance where there is a large stick of a tree with not much foliage at the top.

RESULT
PREVIOUSLY FINE EVERGREEN TREES WILL CONTRIBUTE LESS FOOD FOR INSECTS AND BIRDS DUE TO DISEASE.

DUTCH ELM DISEASE

This continues to exist and prevents English Elm returning to our fields as it was a common presence before the 1970's. Diseases don't disappear, they linger.

RESULT
50 YEARS AFTER LOSING MILLIONS OF TREES WE HAVE NO NATIVE DISEASE RESISTANT VARIETY OF DUTCH ELM.

HORSE CHESTNUT BLEEDING CANKER

This is now present in about half of our trees. It is obvious, leading to the appearance of dead looking leaves after MidSummer and loss of limbs on older trees, leading to Councils removing the trees if they appear to be a danger to others.

RESULT
DOES NOT KILL THE TREE INSTANTLY AND RECOVERY IS SOMETIMES POSSIBLE. HORSE CHESTNUTS SUPPORT 3 TYPES OF INSECT WITH LEAVES BUT ALSO PROVIDE FOOD FOR EARLY BEES IN APRIL.

MASSARIA DISEASE

This affects Plane Trees. Plane trees are often present in towns as they are resistant to pollution. This fungus may mean that trees have to be removed due to risk of falling branches. The consequences of this are that the environment of towns such as London (the London Plane is one name for this tree) will suffer as even one large tree less is a less pleasant environment for everyone. Trees produce oxygen, a valuable commodity in any town.

RESULT
FEWER TREES AND MORE POLLUTION IN TOWNS AS A RESULT OF A FUNGUS DISEASE.

CEDAR BLIGHT

This affects Western Hemlock and Cedar. As both of these are valuable Forestry Crops the potential is there to severely affect Forestry Yields.

RESULT
DISEASES IN FORESTRY TREES LEAD TO ALL PAPER PRODUCTS BEING MORE EXPENSIVE THAN THEY WOULD OTHERWISE BE.

CONCLUSION

So, there are diseases out there, which seem in the case of funguses, to be easily spreading, especially with more humid weather most years in the UK. The impact on insects, especially as a result of the problems with Ash, is going to be more than significant, it is going to be catastrophic. This will also have a devastating effect on birds. In fact the huge decline in bird populations in recent years is already a concern as I outlined in Chapter 1.

There are others out there. **Xylella fastidiosa** is a bacterium which causes disease in grapevine, citrus and olive plants, several species of broadleaf trees widely grown in the UK, and many herbaceous plants. Many Olive Trees in Italy have died from this already. Italy depends on the industry from Olive trees. Oak Trees could be killed if this bacteria gets into the UK. It was almost unknown before 2013 showing how quickly serious environmental change can happen. We need to plant many more trees as whatever happens, severe losses from disease are inevitable.

WHAT CAN WE DO ?

We can help **BIRDS** by feeding them by providing plants in our gardens that provide food for them in the form of berries and seeds. Bird feeders are also good provided they are cleaned on a regular basis.

We can help **INSECTS** by planting trees that support insects where we can. The table overleaf shows trees of the countryside that have insect populations.

We can help **ANIMAL WILDLIFE** by providing suitable habitats which include the increased planting of trees—**we must anticipate major losses in the future.**

TREES OR VERY LARGE SHRUBS FAVOURED BY INSECTS

Lets do a comparison between two extremes...

We have made mistakes in the past. Whilst not so prevalent as they were, in the 1970's Leylandii hedges were planted everywhere in the UK. These grew into huge trees. My garden has a Monterey Cypress (one of the parent plants of Leylandii) and it is now so tall, that at some point, it will be unstable and have to be removed. This does offer shelter for birds. But, not being a native tree to this country, it actually supports only one insect, which also visits Cypresses, and that only on a sporadic basis.

I'm replacing this Monterey Cypress tree, in time. with the oak tree which has been growing for 20 years beneath it. When big enough, this will offer seasonal shelter for birds but will be able to support up to 284 different types of insect. They in turn are used by birds as a food source.

An Oak Tree grows very slowly, so even if a seedling in a small garden will take up to 30 years to have overgrown the space and 11 years before it can produce any other oaks. One of the problems of the march of housing is that Oak Trees have no protection greater than other trees. They really should as the value they provide for wildlife is immense. Build a house AROUND an oak, don't chop it down! Locally there is a "Cedar View Close" There are no cedars anywhere but oak trees were chopped down for the houses. I call it "Felled Oak Close" as that is an accurate description of what happened there and what happens too often in our rush to build houses.

Small trees and shrubs are good to have in a small garden but there is a huge difference to the value for birds and for insects between plants. Plants such as Hawthorn have species of insects that feed on the leaves and they provide some pollen, nectar and berries (and a nesting site) They are very valuable wildlife trees when everything is considered.

The table overleaf relates to the "number of insect species" reported by various studies as being reliant (ie feeding upon) certain trees and shrubs. The figures provided relate to what we have in the UK and these will vary in other countries and even other sources.

After the table there are recommendations for Trees and Shrubs for a small garden.

The maximum number of insect species is not the same as the number of insects (biomass) One insect type could occur in thousands or many species may occur on one tree with just a few of each. Oak trees will never contain 284 species on one tree because of the different temperature zones and habitats of the UK. The research behind this is an amalgam from Southwood, Fairhurst and Soothill and more recent resources, But like insects, statistics will also move around over the coming years!

Tree - Common Name / Latin Name	Insect Species	Food Provided for Insects	Food for Birds	Size of Tree @20 Years	Comments
Oak English and Sessile/ Quercus	284	Leaves	Insects and Nuts	5 Metres	An ecosystem in one tree.
Weeping Willow / Salix	266	Leaves	Insects	14 Metres Height / Spread	Not suitable within 30 metres of houses
Silver Birch / Betula	229	Leaves	Seeds and Insects	9 Metres	Life expectancy 60 -100 years
Hawthorn / Crataegus	149	Leaves Pollen Nectar	Seeds Insects and Berries	5 Metres	Suitable for small gardens. When pruned appropriately, a good nesting site for birds
Poplar/Populus	97	Leaves	Insects	12 metres some species	Not suitable within 30 metres of houses
Crab Apple /Malus	93	Nectar and Pollen. Fruit	Insects and Fruit	4 metres	Suitable for small gardens.
Scots Pine /Pinus	91	Leaves / Cones	Insects / Seeds	7 metres	An unusual choice but good for a medium sized garden
Alder/Alnus	90	Leaves	Insects / Seeds	8 metres	Waterside tree only
Elm/ Ulnus	82	Leaves	Insects Seeds	Dead	Still suffering from Dutch Elm Disease though resistant plants may be available in the future
Hazel/Corylus	73	Leaves / Pollen	Insects Pollen	5 metres	Pollard when it gets too tall suitable for small gardens
Beech/Fagus	64	Leaves	Insects	4 metres	Ok as a hedge in a small garden
Ash /Fraxinus	41	Leaves	Insects	7 metres	Not recommended for planting until we have a variety resistant to the dieback disease
Spruce - Picea	37	Leaves Sap	Insects	6 metres	

Lime -Tilia	31	Leaves Pollen Nectar	Insects	6 metres with similar spread	
Rowan (Sorbus)	28	Leaves - Pollen Nectar	Insects Berries	7 metres	Needs sunny position in a small garden
Hornbeam (Carpinus)	28	Leaves	Insects	4 metres	Can be pruned as a hedge
Field Maple (Acer)	20	Leaves pollen	Insects	4 metres	
Larch (Larix)	17	Leaves	Insects	10 metres	Liable to dieback disease
Gorse (Ulex)	16	Leaves (!)	Cover	4 metres	Not recommended as very prickly plant
Sycamore (Acer)	14	Leaves Pollen	Insects	8 metres	Not for small gardens
Blackthorn or Sloe	10	Leaves - Pollen Nectar	Insects Berries	3 metres	Prickly hedge
Alder Buckthorn	8	Leaves	Insects Berries	3 metres	Small Tree but not pretty
Spindle Tree	7	Leaves Flowers	Berries	3 metres	Suitable for small gardens
Wild Service Tree (Sorbus)	6	Leaves	Insects	4 metres	Suitable for small gardens
Sallow Buckthorn	4	leaves	Insects Berries	4 metres	
Holly (Ilex)	4	Leaves Pollen Nectar	Insects	3 metres	Good Nesting Site
Spanish Chestnut (Castenea sativa)	4	Leaves Pollen Nectar	Insects	7 metres	Large tree native to Europe
Horse Chestnut/ Aesculus	3	Leaves Pollen Nectar	Insects	7 metres	Not for small gardens
Common Box	2			2 metres	
Wild Cherry	1	Nectar (Single Cherries Only)	Fruit	8 metres	Many varieties suitable for small gardens
Yew/Taxus	1	…	…	4 metres	Too poisonous for insects

WHAT CAN WE LEARN FROM THIS TABLE OF INSECTS AND TREES?

In the case of trees, it is clear British Native plants win out in supporting the greatest number of insects as they take up all of the top half of the table. Trees that have been here a few hundred years, such as Sycamore which arrived mainly in the 1700's, mostly support many fewer insects than the natives. Those which are basically poisonous hardly support anything. Unlike the majority of perennials we find in garden centres, native trees offer food in the form of leaves for these insects so are a vital part of supporting life. The insect life is not here, without trees.

Put into blunt practicality, if we had room to plant a Yew Tree or an Oak tree, both of similar ultimate size, then we must choose an Oak tree to support our insects.

Now there is something important to say here, garden centres may import plants from abroad and the plants may not be as suitable for our home grown insects. The trees in this country have evolved slightly differently (to cut a long story short!). So check the plant is **UK grown and sourced** if you are planting any British Native tree.

Most of us don't have room for a large tree. But we can still plant shrubs and smaller trees which benefit insects and birds. So the rest of this chapter is a selection of those plants, with honest positives and negatives stated throughout.

TOP TIP

If you already have an English or Sessile Oak tree in your garden there will be already be seedlings around. Pot them up in September, keep them well watered in Summer and you can keep them in a pot for several years.

Then find a local organisation that is planting trees and give the trees to them when they are big enough. You will be planting a future ecological bird and insect metropolis! Future generations will thank you. Karma will thank you.

Make sure there is a strong upward leading shoot on any plants you grow.

PYRACANTHA - LATIN NAME - PYRACANTHA

TYPICAL FLOWERING PERIOD 10/06—28/06 SYMBOLS >>>**#

POINTS SCORED 60 LARGE SHRUB

Prickly intruder deterrent and one that will make you swear when you have to cut it back to shape as it will tear your sweater or pierce your skin. It will bite you!

For birds, it is brilliant for berries (red and orange berries being more favoured than yellow ones. Don't buy the yellow berried forms). Around midSummer it offers an easy reward to a variety of insects who pollinate the plant. The flowers are bright and white. You could make a corner for this plant which will make a good nest site for birds when big enough, and bushy enough. Recommended varieties available include **"Saphyr Orange/ Rouge", "Red Column"** and **"Orange Glow"**.

TREE COTONEASTER - LATIN NAME- COTONEASTER WATERERI

TYPICAL FLOWERING PERIOD 05/06 - 30/06

SYMBOLS >>>>#~~**

POINTS SCORED 96

After many years this remains one of my favourite trees for a small to medium garden.

It is quite large, mine is 5 x 5 metres and is evergreen in most Winters

You can clip it back if it gets out of bounds, but this restricts the availability of its assets unless you wait until the berries have been eaten. And these plentiful berries may be devoured by redwings, blackbirds and thrushes, to name but a few.

Cotoneaster watereri appears with its white flowers (Top left) and red berries (Lower left).

The flowering period is long for a tree, around a month. All kinds of bees, hoverflies and smaller insects love the flowers.

The best varieties are **"John Waterer"** for the greater number of flowers and berries and **"Cornubia"** Avoid the Yellow berried variety which isn't as good for the birds.   There is a weeping type **Cotoneaster "Hybridus Pendulus"** which is up to 2 metres high and suitable for a smaller garden, great in a corner.

If you require a much smaller plant than that with the same characteristics, go for the herring bone **Cotoneaster horizontalis** described in Chapter 4.

CHINESE ROWAN - SORBUS HUPEHENSIS - FLOWERING PERIOD

15/05– 01/06   SYMBOLS >>> POINTS 50**

The Chinese Rowan has flowers that are attractive to more insects and for longer than the UK Native **(Sorbus aucuparia)** which scores only 30 points

Both trees have berries and are very suitable for the smaller garden. In terms of providing leaves for insects to eat and berries for birds, the native Rowan does win out.

HAWTHORN - LATIN NAME - CRATAEGUS MONOGYNA

TYPICAL FLOWERING PERIOD 04/05—06/06 SYMBOLS >>#*~

POINTS SCORED 58 TREE TO 6 METRES

The Hawthorn is a great all rounder for the smaller garden. As a prickly hedge it provides good cover for nesting birds (when tall enough to be away from cats and other predators) plus it is also an attractive small tree with both flowers for insects and berries for birds. For the majority of years, it is not vastly interesting to bees. It does however provide food from its leaves for up to 149 insect types.

Top Tip

If not grown as a hedge it is a good idea to clip it in such a way as to help birds. Especially as over time it can become quite large. To do this, cut long shoots by three quarters of their length to encourage growth of branches that look like the fingers of a hand the next year. Keep doing this until there is a dense growth of branches that could usefully support a nest.

 Avoid double flowered varieties (**"Pauls Scarlet"** for example) that are too far away from the native variety. The Cockspur Thorn **Crataegus crus-galli** has large flowers (more attractive to bees) large thorns that can inflict a bad injury and large berries that seem too large for the smaller birds. This Hawthorn has beautiful Autumn colour (see below) but you need to acknowledge the potentially dangerous thorns!

BEAUTY BUSH - LATIN NAME-KOLKWITZIA

TYPICAL FLOWERING PERIOD 03/05—14/06 SYMBOLS >>>

POINTS SCORED 37 LARGE SHRUB

The Spring flowering shrub is attractive to bees with its tubular flowers. **"Pink Cloud"** (pictured above) is found at garden centres. This needs a well drained soil and can grow 3 metres. Autumn colour of leaves is a bonus.

STRAWBERRY TREE - LATIN NAME - ARBUTUS UNEDO

TYPICAL FLOWERING PERIOD 25/09—20/10 SYMBOLS >>>

POINTS SCORED 36 EVERGREEN TREE 6M

Provides late interest to bees. The fruits are eaten by birds though are barely edible for us humans. Strawberries are a favourite of mine. This tree does produce fruits that only *look* like a strawberry. The latin name means "I eat one, only" I did, that was quite enough. Native of the west of Ireland and easy to grow but a very dark looking tree.

HOLLY - LATIN NAME - ILEX

TYPICAL FLOWERING PERIOD 25/4 –16/5 SYMBOLS >>>

POINTS SCORED 30 LARGE EVERGREEN TREE

Berries occur where there are male and female plants within range. The flowers are attractive to bees and the berries loved by birds. The tree is slow growing initially but will cast very dense shade and will tolerate shade itself. It is best at the very end of a larger garden in a wildlife corner for that reason. It makes a good nesting site for birds and the tree can be trimmed into shape or cut right back. Don't be tempted by variegated varieties. Food plant of the **Holly Blue butterfly.**

SNOWBERRY - LATIN NAME SYMPHORICARPOS ALBA

SYMBOLS >>>~ POINTS SCORED 57

TYPICAL FLOWERING PERIOD 25/06 —01/09

SYMBOLS >>>~ MAX POINTS SCORED 57 LARGE SHRUB

This used to be planted to provide cover for pheasants. It's a plant for a (large) very shady corner where other things do not grow. A coarse, spreading plant. It is very invasive due to its ability to grow through concrete and cracks in pavements and the difficulty of eradicating once established. Its good for a wild corner and offers flowers that are small but which bees including bumblebees like. Some birds will eat the berries. Not for a small garden and only in mine as I cannot get rid of it.

JAPANESE ANGELICA TREE LATIN NAME ARALIA

TYPICAL FLOWERING PERIOD 20/08—10/10 SYMBOLS >>>**

POINTS SCORED 53 LARGE SHRUB / TREE

Another very prickly customer, the variegated version of the Japanese Angelica Tree **"Variegata"** is less vigorous than the plain **"Elata"** and provides open and attractive flowers towards the end of August and start of September. It grows to about 2 to 3 metres but the spread can be almost as much.

It is very attractive to later bees and to hoverflies but not for a small garden.

LEATHER WOOD - LATIN NAME - EUCRYPHIA X NYMANSENSES

TYPICAL FLOWERING PERIOD 23/08—16/09 SYMBOLS >>>>**#~

POINTS SCORED 86 LARGE SHRUB

A potentially large shrub or tree (to 15 metres) growing quickly which has large, white, single flowers in August / September. These are alive with bees and other insects and are one of the best tree options at that time of year.

It likes a neutral to acid soil though "Nymansay" is said to be more tolerant of lime or chalk than some other related species that are intolerant.

It likes a shady place at the bottom, and a sunny place at the top. It has thick foliage when established that provides cover for birds. Being quite late in the season, it is valuable for foraging insects. In its native Tasmania, honey is produced from this plant. The only negative is that there are no real berries or food for birds and the plant is just dark evergreen leaves for the rest of the year. It is also liable to suffer burning in the sun in a dry hot Summer as it prefers things to be cooler.

IVY - LATIN NAME - HEDERA HELIX

TYPICAL FLOWERING PERIOD 01/09 —01/11 SYMBOLS >>>#*

POINTS SCORED 65 LARGE CLIMBING PLANT

I differ from most in a slight dislike of this plant. It provides late nectar for insects which is great. It provides nesting sites for birds and shelter for insects, is a food plant for the **Holly Blue Butterfly** which is fantastic. It is important for the recently arrived (2001) Ivy Bee Colletes hederae which feeds on the flowers in Autumn. So what is my problem?

Ivy climbs up its host tree. The tendency is for it to weaken its host tree by robbing it of the ability to photosynthesise. This happens by the shading out of, at first lower branches and then the upper branches. This can eventually cause a heavily infested tree to fall from the weight of Ivy, or for it to be sickly.

This is not something I like. I know that it is forbidden by some organisations to manage Ivy at all in our woodlands. I disagree. I think it should be removed at an early stage from healthy trees, whilst allowing it to grow up less healthy trees, only. The healthy trees then provide good leaves for insects, which then support the bird population. I think you can see the insects would rather have food from leaves of a healthy tree without Ivy growing up it.

There you go, argue with me on that point! Pigeons like Ivy berries in Spring.

BLACKTHORN LATIN NAME PRUNUS SPINOSA

TYPICAL FLOWERING PERIOD 20/03—20/04 SYMBOLS >>##

POINTS SCORED 48 SHRUB TO 3 METRES

Prickly and anonymous most of the year. From Mid March to Mid April bright, white blossoms appear and are attractive to insects, including early Brimstone butterflies

The fruits are eaten by birds. Well grown plants offer cover for nesting sites for a variety of birds. It does not cast huge shade so with pruning to raise its crown of thorns it is possible to easily grow other plants beneath it.

WEDDING CAKE TREE LATIN NAME CORNUS CONTROVERSA

TYPICAL FLOWERING PERIOD 04/05 - 29/05 SYMBOLS >>>**

POINTS SCORED 56 MEDIUM PERENNIAL

This takes some years to establish, but it is worth saying that once mature this is the one Cornus (The Latin name for Dogwood) to attract insects, and comparatively early in the year at the start of May. This grows slowly, so it is worthwhile paying more for a larger specimen. Pictured just before flowering, on 4th May

CHAPTER 8 — HOW BEES WORK

Honey Bees and Bumblebees effectively have a coordinated society, different members of the "family" undertake different duties.

The key to the success of the honey bee in producing honey is just how hard they work, together, to collect pollen and nectar from plants.

And this is why the decline in bee populations has a huge potential economic impact as they pollinate over 80% of cultivated crops.

The specific economic value of bees and other pollinators has been measured. £220 million in 1996, £691 million in 2014. By 2020, inflation makes £800 million likely. This is the income of a large PLC company in the UK.

85 per cent of the UK's apple crop and 45 per cent of the strawberry crop need bee pollination. Bees are worth $24 billion in the USA. This particular figure does not include how much we would have to pay out extra, to pollinate plants, including crops, if bees were to die out.

Carder Bee **Bombus pascuorum** on Perennial Sunflower.

Albert Einstein was reported as saying that the human race would not last more than 4 years without bees. If he did say this, it was never written down. But, without food from insect pollination, the inevitable result will be starvation for many and the death of most trees and plants..

As custodians of this planet, how could we oversee the already catastrophic decline of insects including bees, of which the oldest fossil was 100 million years old?

Should we not feel **shame** that we are responsible for this decline? Plants and bees evolved together. They both need each other, plants to produce seeds, bees to keep their colony going. No bees = no plants = no humans?

We are not talking about just the honey bee here. The value of pollinating insects to our Economy as a whole is something we have to consider more than we do. And this is not an exaggeration, before it is too late.

ALL BEES NEED POLLEN AND NECTAR

POLLEN contains between 6% and 28% **PROTEIN** —which contains sugar, vitamins and minerals. It also contains some fat. Protein feeds young bees in the hive.

NECTAR contains between 3% and 80% **SUGAR** which contains protein as a significant other ingredient.

I doubt any of you has opened a pack of sugar and just had that for lunch. It is just too much sugar and is harmful at such high concentrations. So sugar content around 50% is easiest to collect and assimilate for an insect. Above 60% the liquid is dense and more difficult for the insect to suck, considering they use a **proboscis.** This is a bit like a drinking straw through which liquid is sucked through. But insects will still feed on flowers with high sugar levels.

Also bees have to work out when plants release nectar or pollen. Dandelions release in the morning. Chicory plants are closed by the afternoon. There is quite a lot of information that bees have to remember when foraging, which, if you think about it, makes them relatively clever insects. Also different bees have different tongue lengths meaning they feed on (and have preference for) different types of flowers.

HONEYBEES

Almost all honeybees nest in man made hives. A rare sight is a wild colony in a wall or tree. The **Queen** produces **workers and drones** (plus there may be a successor or **Daughter Queen** at some stage) and the queen can live 5 years.

Workers start their lives as housekeeping bees for the first few weeks and they look after the **Queen** and the hive. After this period they have a foraging life during the Summer that is typically just a few weeks. In Winter, they will live for longer as they have to wait for Spring to emerge for initial foraging for the hive, before the **Queen** produces more **Workers**, for the next season of the hive.

This explains why bees tend to go for the same plants during their foraging life, to save energy spent in flying to feeding points. Via a "waggle dance" they can point the direction of good forage to others. The plants in the appendix score more if they flower for more than 21 days for this direct reason. It also makes sense for other insects to have a reliable food source too. The word for this is **constancy.**

Imagine that you are driving on a motorway, starving hungry, and needing fuel for the car. You need to go a very long way to get to the only Service Station, but it is shut. You have no fuel, or food, as a result.

Constancy is relying upon the "service station" being open for your visit or in the case of the honey bee having a reliable food source upon which to feed, collect and return to the hive. So it is for the **Workers.**

Drones have a life of mixed blessings really. As a male bee, they get to mate with the Queen to produce other bees, but then they die after mating and cannot perform any other tasks. They get kicked out of the hives towards the end of the season to die, anyway. You have to feel a bit sorry for the drones.

So what actually is a honey bee? In the UK we have **Apis mellifera** the Western Honey Bee which has been interbred with other species, mostly of European origin. In essence we have this bee as a result of this history, though commercial hives will have different balances of ancestors the bee is essentially the same.

	HONEY BEE FACT FILE
FORAGING DISTANCE	1-3 kms typical, over 5kms is possible. An individual worker bee flies up to 500 miles in a life.
FLYING SPEED	17– 28 KMs per hour, less when carrying pollen home with wings beating at 200 times a second.
AVERAGE LIFETIME AMOUNT OF HONEY PER BEE	A maximum of 1/12th of one teaspoon. So it takes 20,000 to a maximum of 100,000 bees to make a successful hive.
FLYING HOURS TO PRODUCE A POUND OF HONEY	55,000 miles and 2 million flowers with over 22,000 trips with 500 bees involved to produce a pound (454grams) of honey.

BUMBLEBEES

There are 24 species likely to be found in the UK. They need our support even more than honey bees as they are TRUE native, wild, insects. They nest in grassland or holes in the ground such as an abandoned mouse nest. Nests can also be found under sheds, or rarely, in an undisturbed, shady corner of the garden, really out of the way. Bumbles all have an extremely docile temperament and are very unlikely to sting. The nests have up to a few hundred insects only whereas honey bee colonies have many thousands. Tree Bumblebees are as logic would dictate, found nesting in trees.

The Bumblebee colony consists of a **Queen**, who over Winters, alone,

Workers (females) who travel a kilometre or more from the hive to get food.

Males stay in the region of the hive except from late Summer when they emerge to feed on flowers and mate.

There is no need for significant Winter stores, which is why the Bumblebee does not make honey in the traditional sense of the word. The Bumblebee **Queens** for the next year emerge after hibernation in Spring to feed as early as February.   In the nest they will lay **female workers** which, like in the honey bee community, initially help with housekeeping within the nest. The **Queen** will stop producing females once there are enough of them and will then produce males who will search for females, out of the nest.

Tree Bumblebee Bombus hypnorum on Geranium pratense the native Wild Geranium

Commonly seen in gardens all over the UK are the

Red Tailed Bumblebee Bombus lapidarius (pictured page 124) Easy to recognise, an all black bee with a red tail, though males also have a yellow stripe.

Buff Tailed bumblebee Bombus terrestris. They keep a society going through Winter, something recorded only since the 1990's in the South of the UK. White tail has a narrow ginger border at the top.

White tailed Bumblebee Bombus lucorum (picture P124). In Spring the small **"Early Bumblebee"** Bombus pratorum emerges and is recognised by its orange tail in addition to the yellow stripes.

The **Garden Bumblebee** Bombus hortorum is the largest type with white bands on the tail a long black face and a lower buzzing noise than others.

The **Common Carder Bee** Bombus pascuorum is an orangey brown all over (pictured page 120) and the **Tree Bumblebee** pictured above is orange at the front black in the middle and white at the end. It is a shorter, more rotund species than the other bumbles and has only been in the UK since 2001 though this invader has proven harmless to other bees.

BUMBLEBEE FACT FILE	
FORAGING DISTANCE	Up to 1.5 km for the Buff Tail Bumblebee. They run out of energy after less than 40 minutes without food and die at this point.
FLYING SPEED	Slower than honey bees up to 16kms an hour. They also beat their wings 200 times a second like a honey bee, but being heavier this does not get them as far, as quickly.
AVERAGE LIFETIME AMOUNT OF HONEY PER BEE	Bumblebees don't make honey. They have stores of "pots" in which they keep a substance which is "honey like" in a form of larder.
NO OF BEES IN A COMMUNITY	Between 50 and 400 per nest and species dependant. So the amount of stored food is significantly less than for a honey bee.

Identification of similar types is difficult even for experts.

The best thing to help with this is a good identification book. There is a great one published by the **Bumblebee Conservation Trust** called **Bumblebees an Introduction** by Dr Nikki Gammans and others (2017) which combines illustrations and pictures to help you see the differences.

Or, join the **Bumblebee Conservation Trust** on a "Bee Walk" where you can see and identify sometimes rare species whilst seeing beautiful areas of the countryside.

Taking pictures of what you see and meeting with like minded people taking action to try to save Bee Habitats is a fantastic way to spend time.

Red Tailed Bumblebee (Bombus lapidarius) on Chives

White Tailed Bumblebee (Bombus lucorum) on Echinacea.

SOLITARY BEES

These are actually said to be more efficient pollinators than honey bees. Estimates vary but most reliable sources put the number of solitary bee species as around 240-243.

They are solitary creatures as the name suggests. Most of these have no social society they just support themselves and the future generations. Many specialise in particular individual flowers as food plants, which makes them **monoleptic,** rather than **polylectic,** visiting many plants. The majority of all other bees are **polylectic.**

Of the total number of bees it is reported that as many as 90% are solitary bees. Some are so small, we might easily dismiss them as some kind of fly.

LEAF CUTTER BEES (MEGACHILE SPECIES)

Leaf cutter bees cut circular segments of leaves of **Rosa, Wisteria, Leycesteria** and other plants, though the damage rarely has any impact on plant survival. The bee takes these leaves to a hole in wood (or a Bee Hotel as on page 127) and uses this to line and seal the nest so that the larvae of the bees will have a supply of pollen and nectar (sealed within the hole) to feed upon.

Up to 40 pieces of leaf will be used to help the development of just one youngster. Leaf Cutter bees emerge in early Summer of the following year after the larvae have pupated over Winter.

SOLITARY BEE FACT FILE	
FORAGING DISTANCE	Between 300 metres and 1 km. Solitary Bees need sustenance within a close distance of where they hatch out. They have no protection of a hive to go to. Many solitary bees have a preference for flowers of the Daisy family or Pea family.
FLYING SPEED	Some of the larger solitary bees such as the leaf cutter have the capacity to fly up to 20kms per hour so faster than bumblebees.
AVERAGE LIFETIME AMOUNT OF HONEY PER BEE	None. Solitary Bees do not make honey. They collect nectar and pollen on the hairs of the bee abdomen.
NO OF BEES IN A COLONY	Briefly 2 when they mate, and then 1 as the Female does the work for the next generation. It is possible for a few females to use the same nest site and to defend it from intruders in a cooperative way, but that is all.

There are 7 species of Leafcutter Bee in the UK and some of them are very similar in appearance. They are about the size of a typical honey bee. You are most likely to see Megachile centuncularis, the **Patchwork Leaf Cutter Bee**. This has a dark orange underside and ginger edges to the abdomen (pictured page 126)

MASON BEES

Mason Bees emerge early in the season (March to May) which means there can be limited forage plants available. For this reason Dandelions are a good thing in your garden to help these species after they have arrived. Like the Leafcutter bees, some species can use "Bee Hotels" but also will use holes or cracks in old brick walls especially if south facing.

After mating (the males soon die) the eggs will produce adults the following year. So, the female will lay the eggs and provide food for the next generation by sealing in the larvae

not with leaves but with mud or soil. In the UK we will often see the **Red Mason Bee**, Osmia Bicornis (light to dark brown with a hint of a ginger).

OTHER SOLITARY BEES

Moving on from Mason Bees but to continue with the Solitary Bees. The latin name **Andrena (Andrena nitida** pictured page 126) covers over 65 species of the **UK MINING BEES.** These bees all nest in the soil. These mining bees collect pollen on their hind legs.

Tawny mining bee (Andrena fulva) - This bee is in flight from March to June. The females of this species are ginger in colour. They nest in short grass. They leave behind little mounds of soil where they have emerged. Look for a 4mm wide hole at the top of the mound and just steer clear of it for a few weeks. Technically a type of sand bee, they are common in the UK.

Grey Patched Mining bee (Andrena nitida) - This bee is in flight from April to July. Often seen on Dandelions (pictured opposite).

Wool carder bee (Anthidium maculatum).

This bee collects hairs from plants such as **Stachys (Lambs Ears) Verbascum** and **Yarrow** for its nests in holes in cavities, trees and man made structures.

The male bee is aggressive and instead of a sting has a row of spikes on its tail. It will often kill other insects that enter its fiercely guarded territory.

A BEE HOTEL

If you have a bee hotel (pictured left) it will mainly attract **Red Mason Bees** (March) and **Leaf Cutter Bees** (June—July) pictured page 126. **Blue Mason Bees** are also possible visitors from April. The female is a small dark blue / black looking bee with silver hairs at the base of the wings and some faint grey/silver stripes on the abdomen. Or you may see the metallic green (male). Both are only 1 cm in length. **Osmia caerulescens**, to give it the Latin name, will tend to go for smaller holes and they will be sealed with a random mixture of sawdust and a dark coloured purple leaf mash, prepared by the bee.

Bees that use Bee hotels are found less often, the further north you go in the UK. So it might be a good idea to check if you do have these bees in your area, before buying a hotel that might only otherwise be used by spiders.

In my case the **Leaf Cutter Bees** and **Mason Bees** very quickly found my hotel

Bee Hotel—Notice the top row with two leaf cutter bee holes (left) and then two mason bee holes

but for success you need to bear in mind the following.

Siting of a hotel is important, it should be hung on a wall or fence over a metre above the ground and slightly sloping down, so that rain does not get into the holes. Away from prevailing wind if possible.

Type— Avoid narrow hotels or those without a good roof. If rain gets into the holes over Winter this is one of the key causes of failure. Some examples are very poorly made and will not last.

Duration Unless you have the type (as pictured) where you can clean out the cells completely, by taking it apart, hotels with holes in wood only last for two years before the hygienic conditions and parasites become an issue. Remember we want healthy colonies, and the natural way is that these bees will use different sites every year. So a hotel is not a cheap option!

Cheaper Alternative. If you have a bamboo plant or a **Leycesteria** (Pheasant Bush) you can actually make a free hotel by tying tubes together (but make sure each one has only one end open, which is possible if you cut the stems in that way) Or even better, find some wood, drill holes in it, and hang it up noting the comment about a solid end to the holes which should be at least 10—15 centimetres deep and you MUST have a good watertight roof to your hotel.

The young bees in the hotel will hatch out next Spring. It is worth noting these bees are totally harmless and safe (and educational) for children. In fact apart from seeing them hatch out and fly, you will hardly notice them at all apart from when they visit your flowering plants, and your hotel, of course!

CUCKOO BEES

Cuckoo Bees are **parasitic.** They rely on the host bee to provide all the food for the next generation. About 25% of all solitary bees are Cuckoo bees.

Bumblebees mostly have a Cuckoo bee for each of the species.

These are of similar enough appearance that they do not get attacked by the host species. They then lay eggs within the host colony which use the host bee as food for the larvae. The bee then hatches out and the process starts again. Whilst not a pleasant aspect of nature, it is our duty to live and let live. All these creatures have a place in the natural order of things and cuckoo bees are as good at pollinating as other bees.

Other insects such as Leaf Cutter Bees have similar parasitic insects who lay eggs within a colony or larvae case, in much the same way as a Cuckoo lays its egg in the nest of another bird. Populations of cuckoo bees are much lower than the host bumblebees and extinction of them is a real possibility.

THE BRAMBLE BEE CERATINA CYANEA

There are many examples of smaller solitary bees that tuck themselves out of the way. The bramble bee is a small, silver blue bee which lays eggs within a bramble plant, it overWinters within there, hatching out in the Spring. There are many similar "aerial nesters" among solitary bees. In a garden, we keep brambles under control but with other plants leaving areas undisturbed is only positive for insects.

HAIRY FOOTED FLOWER BEE

Anthophora plumipes, or the Hairy Footed Flower Bee is found south of the Peak District in the main and is common in gardens.

This species is one that visits my Lungwort, (Pulmonaria) each Spring. In fact it likes that plant in preference to almost anything else. Females are black and males are sandy colour with darker stripes. They fly very quickly and buzz quite loudly, two ways of getting accurate identification.

They are very unlikely to stop still enough for a photo at any time. They nest in areas of clay, mud and areas of old cob walls.

This chapter (and the next one) are both a toe, dipped into the water of a huge, complex subject. It is a summary with a broad brush. I hope this will get you interested in finding out more!

Sources of information with regard to insects are liable to contradict themselves but on the Internet I recommend the following.

bumblebeeconservation.org The place to go for everything bumblebee related.

BWARS.org (Bees wasps ants recording society) Shows areas where insects are recorded.

butterfly-conservation.org Beautifully presented source of information about butterflies and moths.

ukmoths.org Has an incredible record of different moths species and photos.

CHAPTER 9 —
BUTTERFLIES AND OTHER INSECTS

In this chapter we cover moths, butterflies, hoverflies, dragonflies and the rest!

Comma Butterfly on **Allium**

The scope of this book up to this point related to plants in our gardens that can feed insects with pollen and nectar. Moths are included with the butterflies in the scores allocated to plants and like butterflies they feed on nectar, not pollen, but will also feed on windfall fruit and tree sap.

Most butterfly attractive species of plant are also attractive to moths. However there is a lot I feel we don't know about these night creatures. I would need to camp out every night for the next two years in a moth metropolis for me to bring you the same standard of results as for the other day flying insects in this book.

For this chapter we are looking at the plants that Insects use as food plants in the larval or youngster stage. The life cycle of a moth is essentially, egg on food plant, caterpillar stage, pupae or chrysalis (often over Winter) and then moth. As a result of the focus on food plants this chapter is in a different format, a list of the insects with the plants they are associated with, when and where they are most likely to be found. See the key below that explains the results.

Area found	S W C N FN	South ,West Central, North, Far North (Scotland)	Fields or Wood Habitat
Time of Day	Day	Dusk	Night
Population Status	RARE	VULNERABLE	COMMON

MOTHS—CREATURES (MOSTLY) OF THE NIGHT

So where do moths fit in with the food chain? Moths are important for maintaining bat populations as so many of them are **crepuscular** (only coming out at night) just like bats. Birds also rely on them for food and will find both hiding moths and caterpillars, during the day. Moths are prey to a lesser extent to other insects but also to spiders, frogs, toads, lizards, shrews and hedgehogs who also like moths as food.

Moths are also pollinating insects like butterflies are. Its just you may not see them actually doing it, though many moths eat nothing during their lives. Sustaining populations of moths is important, but studies have recorded significant declines (over 40% in 40 years to 2013 and more since). There are 2500 species of moth but there will be extinctions. I have selected for my table, some of those that are most likely to be found in the UK. For simplicity I have used the common names of the moths.

MOTH COMMON NAME	3	4	5	6	7	8	9	10	S	W	C	N	FN	DAY	DUSK	NIGHT	FOODPLANTS
RARE															▒	■	
VULNERABLE																	
COMMON																	
Deaths Head Hawk Moth					■	■	■		▒							■	Potato Leaves
Convolvulus Hawk Moth					■	■	■		▒							■	Wild Bindweed
Privet Hawk Moth				■	■				▒							■	Privet
Lime Hawk Moth			■	■					▒							■	Lime
Eyed Hawk Moth			■	■	■				▒							■	Willow / Apple
Poplar Hawk Moth			■	■	■				▒	▒						■	Willow/ Poplar
Bee Hawk Moth			■	■					▒					■			Honeysuckle/ Bedstraw
Elephant Hawk Moth			■	■	■				▒							■	Epilobium (Willowherb)
Emperor Moth	■	■	■						▒					■			
Puss Moth		■	■	■					▒						▒	■	Willow Poplar
Sallow Kitten		■	■	■					▒							■	Pussy Willow
Swallow Prominent		■	■		■				▒	▒						■	Poplar/ Willow
Coxcomb Prominent			■		■				▒	▒	▒					■	Willow/ Birch/ Alder Poplar & Willow
Buff Tip			■	■	■				▒	▒	▒					■	Hazel/ Oak / Sallow
Lobster Moth			■	■					▒	▒						■	Hazel /Oak/ Beech
Oak Hook Tip			■		■				▒	▒						■	Oak
Peach Blossom			■	■	■				▒	▒					▒	■	Bramble
Large Yellow Underwing			■	■	■				▒	▒	▒					■	Primroses
Red Underwing					■	■			▒	▒							Poplar/ Willow
Cabbage Moth		■	■	■	■				▒						▒	■	Pests of Brassicas
Turnip Moth		■	■	■	■				▒							■	Pests of Turnips
Brown Tail Tussock*			■	■					▒	▒					▒		Has been a Pest in the past
Yellow Tail Tussock*				■	■				▒	▒						■	Oak/ Hawthorn/ Birch/ Blackthorn
Vapourer				■	■	■			▒	▒							Hawthorn
Blairs Shoulder Knot		■	■						▒							■	Monterey and other Cypress
Wormwood Pug		■	■						▒	▒	▒					■	Artemsia (Wormwood)
Burnished Brass			■	■					▒	▒	▒				▒		Nettles and Echium
Common Footman			■	■	■				▒	▒	▒					■	Lichen bark on Oak
Muslin Moth		■	■	■					▒	▒	▒					■	Dandelion Dock Chickweed
Large Emerald		■	■	■					▒	▒	▒					■	Birch Hazel Beech
Winter Moth pest of apples	■						■		▒								Winter season only
Currant Moth pest of currents				■					▒	▒						■	Hazel Hawthorn Sloe

MOTH COMMON NAME	3	4	5	6	7	8	9	10	S	W	C	N	FN	DAY	DUSK	NIGHT	FOODPLANTS
RARE															▨	■	
VULNERABLE																	
COMMON																	
Oak Beauty	■	■							▨	▨	▨					■	Oak Birch Lime
Peppered Moth		■	■	■	■	■			▨		▨	▨				■	Oak Birch Beech
Brindled Beauty	■	■							▨	▨	▨					■	Birch Oak Beech
Common Pug			■	■	■				▨	▨	▨						Hawthorn Bramble
Foxglove Pug			■	■	■				▨		▨						Foxglove
Garden Carpet			■	■	■	■	■		▨		▨						Cabbage Wallflowers
Lace Border				■	■					▨	▨						Thyme Marjoram
Sycamore Moth				■	■	■			▨		▨					■	Sycamore
Silver Y			■	■	■	■	■		▨		▨	▨		■	▨		Wide range of plants
Garden Tiger					■	■			▨		▨						Deadnettle
Cream Spot Tiger			■	■					▨		▨						Plaintain
Scarlet Tiger				■	■				▨		▨					■	Nettles/Docks/Brambles
Lappet Moth				■	■	■			▨		▨						Hawthorn Apple
Cinnabar Moth inedible to birds			■	■	■				▨		▨						Ragwort
White Ermine distasteful to birds			■	■	■				▨		▨	▨					
Buff Ermine	■	■	■	■	■				▨		▨	▨	■			■	Dandelions Docks
Cream Wave			■	■	■				▨		▨						Bedstraw Dock
Grey Pine Carpet				■	■	■	■		▨		▨					■	Scots Pine
Barred Yellow			■	■					▨		▨				▨	■	
6 Spotted Burnet				■	■	■			▨		▨			■			Birds Foot Trefoil
Poisonous and rejected by birds. Like all burnets																	
Common Swift			■	■	■	■			▨		▨				▨		Pest of barley and wheat
Ghost Swift				■	■				▨		▨				▨		up to three years below ground
Emperor Moth	■	■							▨		▨				▨	■	Purple Loosestrife
Kentish Glory	■	■										▨					Birch
Codling Moth				■	■												Pest
Pea Moth				■	■												Pest
Green Oak Tortrix Moth				■	■				▨		▨				▨	■	Sycamore / Beech
Leaf Mining Moths			■	■	■												Hawthorn
Orange Underwing	■	■							▨		▨						Birch
Speckled Yellow			■	■					▨		▨						Deadnettles/Woundwort
Burnet Companion			■	■	■				▨		▨						Birds Foot Trefoil

131

MOTH COMMON NAME	3	4	5	6	7	8	9	10	S	W	C	N	FN	DAY	DUSK	NIGHT	FOODPLANTS
RARE															�	■	
VULNERABLE																	
COMMON																	
Oak Lutestring						■			■		■				■		Oak
Brimstone Moth		■	■	■	■	■			■		■						Hawthorn
Feathered Thorn				■	■	■	■	■	■		■						Oak & Hawthorn
Swallow Tailed Moth				■	■				■		■						Hawthorn

* Irritant

Key to Moth Tables on previous pages

Consider which of these plants you have or want to have in your garden and how they could be helping moths *if they are found in your area.* Plants that are **not desirable** to plant in your garden from this table are **Bramble, Bindweed, Rosebay Willowherb, Ragwort. Stinging Nettles** are up to you!

Also, based upon where the moths can be found, some trees provide essential support for these moths. Used in conjunction with the table in Chapter 7 you can see the basis for some of my small garden tree recommendations. For example, **Hawthorn** can be controlled as a small tree in a small garden, but is valuable for a wide range of wildlife including moths mentioned in this table.

Do not touch any caterpillars on Oak Trees if the **Oak Processionary Moth** is reported in your area. Even airborne hairs from this caterpillar cause an extreme reaction on skin. Check local information on where these caterpillars are.

MOTHS AND LIGHT POLLUTION

Moths are being killed by lighting, so consider this when one enters your bedroom of a night and flies around a light. Switch all lights off as quickly as possible and open the window, It will initially be blinded but after a while will find its way out. If you leave the light on, the moth will be fried by the heat of the bulb. We should be considering cold external lighting to avoid killing moths (and other insects). Not to mention the mental confusion moths suffer from. When is night day? When is day night? Light pollution marches up at 2% every year overall (Chris Kyba German Research Centre) and is considered one of many causes of moth depopulation. We need to reverse the trend.

POLLINATION

Moths often prefer white or yellow flowers that are fragrant. The combination of these two aspects means plants are easier to find over night. In most other aspects, Moths like similar flowers to butterflies, and this is reflected in the results in the appendix .Not all are crepuscular, some moths such as the Hummingbird Hawkmoth pollinate by day.

BUTTERFLIES—BEAUTIFUL WORKS OF ART

Here follows a table of butterflies, food plants and information about when and where you are likely to see them. This is the key to the table.

Area found	S W C N FN	South ,West Central, North, Far North (Scotland)	Migrant or Summer Visitor
Population Status	RARE	VULNERABLE	COMMON

BUTTERFLY															
Months of Main Activity	**3**	**4**	**5**	**6**	**7**	**8**	**9**	**10**	**S**	**W**	**C**	**N**	**FN**	**Main Foodplant**	**Comments**
Orange Tip Butterfly		■	■	■					▨	▨	▨			Cuckoo Flower	20 Day life expectancy
														Garlic Mustard	Food Plant easy to grow
Small Skipper					■				▨	▨	▨			Yorkshire Fog	20 Day life expectancy
														Timothy	Needs grassy meadow
Large Skipper				■	■				▨	▨	▨			False Brome	Butterfly for 3 weeks, caterpillar <11 months
														Cocksfoot	
Grizzled Skipper				■		■			▨					Barren Strawberry	Vulnerable to expansion of London Green Belt
														Silverweed	Only lives 15 days or so
															Down 50% since 1970's
Large White		■	■	■	■	■			▨	▨	▨			Nasturtiums	Even these common butterflies are much
Small White			■	■	■	■			▨	▨	▨			Cabbage Family	less common than they used to be
Green Veined White	■	■	■	■	■	■			▨	▨	▨			Hedge and	Likes Ditches and Damp Fields
														Garlic Mustard	Lives 30 days
Wood White			■		■				▨	▨				Vetch	Feeds on Bugle and Ragged Robin for nectar
															Vulnerable down 62%
Brimstone		■	■		■	■	■		▨				▨	Buckthorn	Life expectancy up to one year
														Alder Buckthorn	The one butterfly we can help in our garden
															Likes Primroses to feed
Clouded Yellow			▨	▨	▨	▨	▨							Trefoil Meliot	Migrant
Pale Clouded Yellow		▨	▨	▨	▨	▨	▨								Migrant only
Small Tortoiseshell	■	■	■	■	■	■			▨					Stinging Nettles	Butterflies over Winter in sheds
Peacock		■	■	■	■				▨					Stinging Nettles	or similar places
Painted Lady		▨	▨	▨	▨	▨	▨	▨						Visit flowers	A migrant that cannot
														for nectar	survive cold Winters
Comma		■	■	■	■	■			▨					Hop, Willow	
														Leaves and Nettles	
Red Admiral		▨	▨	▨	▨	▨	▨		▨					Eggs Laid on	A migrant which has a resident generation
														Nettles	after mid Summer
White Admiral				■					▨					Honeysuckle	
Marsh Fritillary			■	■					▨				▨	Food plant is	Vulnerable in Europe
														Devils Bit Scabious	Down 46% since 1970's

BUTTERFLY															
Months of Main Activity	3	4	5	6	7	8	9	10	S	W	C	N	FN	Main Foodplant	Comments
Small Pearl Bordered Fritillary				■	■				▦			▦	▦	Eggs laid on wild violets	
Dark Green Fritillary			■	■	■				▦					Dog Violets	
High Brown Fritillary				■	■				▦			▦	▦	Violets	80% down since 70's
Duke of Burgundy Fritillary			■	■					▦	▦	▦			Eggs laid on Primrose	Few habitat sites
														and Cowslip	
Common Blue			■	■	■	■	■		▦	▦				Eggs laid on	
														Birds Foot Trefoil	
														Clover and Restharrow	
														Black Medick	
Meadow Brown				■	■	■	■		▦	▦				Grasses with finer leaves such as Briza Media, Quaking Grass.	Probably our most common butterfly the very symbol of a meadow
														Festuca	
Gatekeeper					■	■			▦	▦				Lays eggs on Couch Grass	
														Meadow Grass	
Small Heath			■	■	■	■			▦	▦				Food plant	Over winters in grass
														is grass	
Ringlet				■	■				▦	▦				Food plant	Increasing populations
														grass species	Over winters in grass
The Wall		■	■	■	■	■			▦	▦				grasses in	Butterfly lives about 20 days. Down 38% since the 1970's
														areas such as	
														quarries, railway	
														embankments	
Speckled Wood		■	■	■	■	■			▦	▦				Food plants	Showing some good recovery in populations
														is grass,	Lives 20 days or so
														Yorkshire fog	
														and couch grass	
Marbled White					■	■			▦	▦				Red Fescue	
														Yorkshire fog	
Chalk Hill Blue				■	■				▦					Horseshoe Vetch	Both these blues have
Adonis Blue															similar requirements
Brown Argus			■	■	■				▦					Erodium	Rock Rose and Storks bill easily grown in gardens
															but it has to be the wild
														Helianthemum	flower form of the plant

BUTTERFLY														
Months of Main Activity	3	4	5	6	7	8	9	10	S	W	C	N	FN	Main Foodplant	Comments
Holly Blue														Spring eats leaves	Holly Blue can be supported by us gardeners
														flower of Holly	By having a holly tree
														Autumn eats leaves	(if there is room) from
														Leaves of Ivy	a self sown seedling
															from a local wood is the best result for caterpillars
Black Hairstreak														Eggs are laid on Blackthorn	Likely extinction, yet its food plant is common
Silver Washed Fritillary														Food plant is	Coming back after severe decline in S England
														Violets	
Brown Hairstreak														Food plant is Blackthorn	Eggs laid on sloe but take a year to become
															butterflies needs undisturbed situation and
															vulnerable
															to hedge cutting
Green Hairstreak														Food plant is Broom /Gorse	OverWinters in leaf litter
														Bramble	
Purple Hairstreak														Food plant is Oak	Look at the top of oak trees to get a glimpse
Small Copper														Food Plant is Sorrel	Lives about a month

KEY TO BUTTERFLY TABLES

The way to use the results of the previous pages is as follows. Just consider which of the food plants you have or want to have in your garden and how they could be helping butterflies, provided the area they are in matches the area you are in.

The plants that are **not desirable** to plant in your garden from this table are **Gorse and Nettles though if you have space the latter can be managed.**

The life cycle of a butterfly is that they either emerge from hibernation or hatch out from leaf litter or the soil in Spring. They then mate, lay eggs on a chosen food plant for the next generation. Many of them die after only a month or so, others overWinter. The life expectancy is shown, where notable, on the previous pages.

Food plants (which include trees) are therefore essential to support Butterflies.

Used in conjunction with the table in Chapter 7 you can see the basis for some of my small garden tree recommendations. If you can also draw your own conclusions and make your own choices then you have become an ecologist, someone working out the best result for the local environment. Congratulations!

For example, you might choose to plant Blackthorn which can be controlled as a small (but very prickly) tree or shrub in a small garden, but is valuable for a wide range of wildlife including that mentioned in this book.

GRASSES

Notice the food plants for butterflies include grasses. You can get seed mixes for your grass, or meadow, that include the wonderfully titled "Yorkshire Fog" or "Red Fescue" that will be sources of food for young caterpillars. Choose this grass for your meadow, to help the butterflies.

SHELTER

Butterflies are cold blooded and rely on the warmth of the sun, so for a meadow, or indeed for plants in a garden situation, make sure the position is not too exposed. Most smaller gardens with a hedge or fencing will at least go some way to offer shelter they want if it is a position of sunshine.

To prevent a butterfly "flutterby" plant recommended plants from this book for them to feed upon. The provision of food plants for them will help them stay in your garden.

FOOD

Butterflies want, mainly, nectar, the proboscis is built for sucking up liquid. Those plants that produce nectar have **nectaries** where sugary substances are produced are the best for them. However not all butterflies can access this food. Small butterflies have shorter tongues and find it difficult to feed on a plant such as a buddleia, which has nectar at the end of a long tube. This is why a variety of garden plants is needed.

HOVERFLIES—MASTERS OF MIMICRY

Hoverflies are often ignored or misunderstood but they are fascinating creatures. There are about 270 species in the UK. They range from tiny creatures that look like flies to insects that look a little like bees or wasps, though hoverflies lack the fluffiness (mostly) that bees have. This is known as **"Batesian Mimicry".** The idea is, if I look like a wasp, perhaps I am, so will you mess with me if I can sting you?

Hoverflies are also completely harmless. They do a lot of good in your garden. If you don't have a problem with aphids, then that is down to your local hoverflies. The eggs are like tiny rugby balls, laid near a plant they hope will feed the small creature that hatches out and feeds on aphids or thrips.

Adult hoverflies are common in gardens but face the same dangers as other insects from pesticides. Ironically if you treat your plants to kill aphids, you will also kill the natural predator that eat aphids. This is the crass stupidity of relying on chemicals to kill things when nature can actually do the job for you given some patience. If you can do one thing for hoverflies, then keep the chemicals away. Save money and save our insects!

Hoverfly, having lunch on a single Dahlia pretending to be a little wasp!

HOVER FLY FACT FILE	
POLLINATING ABILITY	More efficient pollinators than butterflies, and good at pollinating small flowers.
FLYING SPEED	Some can reach 12.5 km/h for a very short period. They are easy to identify as hoverflies as they actually "hover". They have two wings not four.
AVERAGE LIFETIME	Very short, the creatures go from egg to larva to pupa to adult in around a month. They overwinter as pupa or in folds of trees as adults.
WHAT PLANTS DO THEY LAY EGGS ON ?	Eggs are laid on plant stems where they think aphids will be. Another good reason to leave tidying up in the garden during the growing season.

3 COMMON HOVERFLIES
EPISERPHUS BALTEATUS – MARMALADE HOVERFLY

Known as the "Marmalade" Hoverfly this is a small very common hoverfly in gardens. The key identification being from dark orange stripes on the abdomen.

CHRYSOTOXUM CAUTUM LARGE WASP HOVERFLY

Like a larger version of "Elegans" pictured on the previous page.

VOLUCELLA PLUMATA BEE HOVERFLY

Sounds like a bee with a high pitched buzz like a hairy footed flower bee. Looks a little like a tree bumblebee with its white tail, but has two wings and the distinctive hoverfly face. Often found in gardens feeding from plants just like a small bumblebee.

TOP TIP

Go out with your mobile phone and try and take snaps of insects outside your door, and on your plants. Look up what you have seen in a good identification book. You will be surprised at what you find!

CONCLUSION

In this chapter we have so far explored plant associations with insects where they feed on leaves during the caterpillar stage. **What of the other insects?** There are 20,000 insect types in the UK. How can I cover all these, dear reader, and keep your attention? Well, firstly, many insects have no associations with plants. We have already addressed those flowers which are greatly attractive to flies or wasps within these pages and in the results. I have to draw the line somewhere, so I'm not going down to the level of an ant. The other insects appreciate the better scoring flowers in this book. Flower beetles, for example appreciate open flowers with rewards that are easy to access.

The table that follows is a brief mopping up exercise for common types of insect left undescribed in this book. The key follows, after the table. Most of our birds feed on insects, and they may not always have a particular preference as long as they (or baby birds) have lunch. **So we have to support the lives of all insects to support the rest of the food chain.**

So don't treat a fly as something to kill, just because it isn't attractive or useful to you!

I, like others, feel that we have to keep planting native trees such as stated in Chapter 7 and native food plants in order to maintain insect populations. After this support at the junior stage of food plants, we help immensely by planting the best plants we can find for our gardens to provide nectar and pollen.

In the next chapter, I talk about my wildlife pond, and plants suitable for ponds and how that will make a difference for insects, and all wildlife in your area, with a special feature on one of my favourite insects, the dragonfly.

Insect - Common Name	3	4	5	6	7	8	9	10	S	W	C	N	FN	Feeds on plants in	Prey on insects in	Larva develop in	Food Plants
Emperor Dragonfly														GHP	GHP	P	
Common Hawker														HP	HP	P	
Broad Bodied Chaser														GHP	GHP	P	
Banded Demoiselle														R	R	P	
Blue Tailed Damselfly														GP	GP	P	
Common Darter														GP	GP	P	
Common Blue Damselfly														GHP	GHP	P	
Large Red Damselfly														P	P	P	
Field Grasshopper																	
Mayfly																PR	
Earwig														GH		GH	
Pied Shield Bug														GH		GH	Deadnettle
Green Shield Bug														GHW			Will eat garden plants
Common Frog Hopper														GHW		GHCW	Source of cuckoo spit
Giant Lacewing														GH		GH	They eat aphids
Alderfly														P	P	P	
Seven Spot Ladybird														GHW	GHW	GHW	In danger from foreign invader
Bee Fly														GH	GH	H	Parasite of Solitary Bees
Common Hoverfly														GHW			Episyrphus Balteatus
Wasp Hoverfly														GHW			Chrysotoxum cautum
Cockchafer														GHW		HW	Crop Pest - Larvae develop for 3 years

Feeding on plants in...
Prey on insects in...
Larvae develop in...

KEY

G) Gardens
H) Hedgerows and Fields
W) Woods
P) Ponds
R) Rivers

DRAGONFLY FACT FILE	
POLLINATING ABILITY	Sometimes pollinate plants but they are looking (with their 360 degree vision) for insects to eat
FLYING SPEED	Speeds of 40 km/h are not uncommon reaching a maximum of around 60km/h
AVERAGE LIFETIME	Up to 4 years as a larvae in a pond, a month at most flying around as a Dragonfly
WHAT PLANTS DO THEY LAY EGGS ON	Eggs are laid on plant stems in ponds or vegetation on the edge of ponds
WHAT IS THE PURPOSE OF DRAGONFLIES?	In areas infested with mosquitos, the dragonfly is a significant predator in managing populations. They are food for many birds, such as the **Hobby**

CHAPTER 10—MY WILDLIFE POND

DRAGONFLIES, DAMSELFLIES AND HOW TO MAKE YOUR POND WORK FOR THEM
Ever since the days when as a child I was lucky to always had a pond in my garden. As a teenager I hatched out **Emperor Dragonflies** and **Broad Bodied Chaser** from a pond of only 350 gallons (1324 litres) .Well that was when we realised what the larvae were. The creatures that hatch out as dragonflies look like mini dinosaurs or space monsters. I have a special love for these harmless creatures but they are difficult to support in a pond. Here are some hints.

1)   Buy pond plants from a supplier who has them in the open, there are more than likely eggs within the plant. This may produce a dragonfly that prefers a river setting, so those will fly away and not come back or one that will stay around the pond. The negatives are that you don't know what other life might appear, so there is no control over things like flatworms.

2)   Rely on visiting Dragonflies, who will lay eggs in stems of pond plants—so avoid cutting these back if it looks as if eggs have been laid. Patience! They also need smooth plants to emerge on, such as bullrush or yellow flag iris.

3)   Goldfish are not compatible with Dragonflies, or indeed any other insect life you will find in a pond. Dragonflies love frog tadpoles, and too many fish will pretty much clean them up from a pond robbing the larvae of food.

4)   Now this is difficult. You need to protect Dragonflies when they emerge from the pond. They are incredibly vulnerable to predation, and to not transforming correctly. You might have to get up at 5AM or so in the morning, to sit there whilst others emerge. It is though one of the most rewarding experiences of my life, seeing this mini monster hatch out into a dragonfly.

But if you don't do it, a bird will most likely eat the emerging dragonfly or a local cat may decide to play with it. Fencing plus a grill up to a metre in height, but crucially without any sharp edges as wings are easily damaged, may help this. The larvae is up to four years in a pond, such an ending to a life in the beak of a bird sits uncomfortably with me. Do you not have a responsibility as a pond owner to support your wildings?

5)   An alternative is, remove some larvae from the pond, include tadpoles or offer small pieces of raw meat tied with string if there is no natural food in the pond, into a large 1 metre container full of pond water and out of way of birds. Include bulrush stems for them to climb up , and keep monitoring!

Damselflies and smaller dragonflies tend to be harder for predators to spot when they hatch out, so you are more likely to have success with the species such as **Common Blue Damselfly** and smaller **Red Dragonfly** Sympetrum fonscolombii which will find you in most areas of the UK.

PROTECTING WILDLIFE

My garden, whilst in the suburbs of London nevertheless has frogs, toads and two species of newt that use the pond every year. And the reason they are there is largely due to the developing insect life within the pond. Whilst frog tadpoles for example start up by feeding on algae they move to eating larvae of gnats or mosquitos and move on to anything non vegetarian. I remember putting little pieces (less than a cm square) of raw meat in the pond on a string for a few hours, watching the tadpoles crowd around to feed on the nutrients provided. They are definitely not vegetarians! Providing the right water quality is important. A PH testing kit is helpful and a level around 7 is perfect.

Very small creatures such as **mayfly** larvae and **daphnia** species need clear water to survive and in the case of mayfly, to hatch out from the pond. Frogs and toads will help your wildlife garden by eating at least some of the slugs that damage your plants, though they will never, in my experience, eat enough! But we have to do certain things to make the best of a wildlife pond, so the next pages are about avoiding traps that many pond owners can fall into which can make a pond a disaster zone.

THE RIGHT POND FOR WILDLIFE—AVOIDING PITFALLS

My preference is for a preformed liner which is often made from fibreglass or high density polyethylene. This should be a minimum of 1400 litres, go to more if you can but, more importantly it must have significant shallower shelves (around 20 cms and often known as planting shelves) as well as one deep area (over 50 cms). A number of ponds available have no shelves. Tadpole development is extremely vulnerable in the early stages, and it is easier for them to rest on a planting shelf overnight than fall down into the mud at the bottom.

The shallower area will warm up quicker in the morning sun. The advantages of preformed liners are that invasive water plants will not damage the pond and can be removed easily. It is harder, however, to dig the original hole and get the pond to be level. Time and preparation is the only way to ensure this is done correctly. A butyl liner pond is easier to dig within an area and will look more in place. However you must avoid any invasive water plants whose roots can puncture a liner and cause leaks (such as bullrushes). The importance of having carpet or something else significant below the liner to cushion it is vital.

It is a great idea to have a pre formed or liner based waterfall coming down into any pond. For birds and other wildlife there should be 2—6 centimetres of water that stays there when the water is not coming down the waterfall. This makes a useful bird bath and source of drinking water and the shallow edges (0—3 centimetres) enable insects to also, easily, drink water without risking death by drowning. Even if you have no room for a pond a small dish part filled with stones can be a valuable source of drinking water for insects. They can land on the stones and drink the water without the risk of drowning.

If you have any tadpoles, you should not use a circulating water pump until the baby amphibians are froglets or newtlets. With an unprotected intake the pump will produce tadpole fatalities, not what you want with a wildlife pond. I advocate a solar powered pump with a solar panel to provide power. This is a more gentle type of pump than an electrical sourced one. A fabric filter can also allay casualties. Another alternative is just to top up the pond every week via a hose and the waterfall, this will disturb the wildlife within much less than an electrical pump.

For insects purity of water and oxygen within the water is important. The problem is usually that too many nutrients are washed into the pond producing bindweed (a long stringy grass like substance that blocks up ponds) which will inhibit insect development and actually kill larvae. It has to be removed. Buy oxygenating pond weed to help the water condition, such as Canadian pond weed **Elodea canadensis**.(and note this has to be this latin name not other Elodea types)

Something that affects our waterborne insect populations is the amount of invasive water plants we have imported from abroad. These cause the same loss of habitat as invasive land borne plants. Let us explore these nightmare plants....

ALIEN INVADERS—BANNED WATER PLANTS

Since 2014 there has been legislation that bans the sale of the following. Any retail establishment that sells these plants is liable for a £5000 fine and a person can serve up to 6 months in jail.

Parrots Feather (Myriophillum brasiliensis) - This forms mats of feathery vegetation in and out of water that crowd out all other plants. Often used to be sold at garden centres.

Australian (Or New Zealand) Swamp stonecrop - Latin name Crassula helmsii. My local pond has been fighting a 20 plus year battle with this short plant that looks like land based stonecrop. It grows in water and land and completely out competes everything. It will deplete water of oxygen, destroy all life, and even if removed, a 1 millimetre piece can regenerate and start the infestation again.

This plant is spreading its doom through the UK and is a real concern for the future of our water way habitats as it cannot be eradicated.

Water fern and Azolla filiculoides—both also banned.

THE CONSEQUENCES OF PLANTING THESE PLANTS ARE DEATH TO AQUATIC LIFE INSECTS AND REMOVAL OF HABITAT AND FOOD SOURCES

The Government already spends £1.8 Billion a year clearing invasive plants from British waterways. Money that if the plants were not here could be spent elsewhere. As much as anything, this demonstrates why we have to be careful what we plant. Also listed

Floating primrose willow (*Ludwigia peploides*)

Water hyacinth *(Eichhornia crassipes)*

Cabomba *(Cabomba caroliniana)*

Curly waterweed (*Lagarosiphon major* often inaccurately called *Elodea crispa*)

American skunk cabbage (*Lysichiton americanus*)

Alligator weed (*Alternanthera philoxeroides*)

Nuttall's waterweed (*Elodea nuttallii*)

Giant Rhubarb (*Gunnera tinctoria*)

Garden Centres and Internet establishments still sometimes sell these plants, despite this being against the Law. A word of warning, many OTHER water plants are being imported from all corners of the globe, and many of them could turn out to be as invasive as the ones above, once introduced in this country.

The reason for the concern is that roots and plantlets have no limit within water. So for the pond, either non invasive or controllable plants are recommended only. And native plants are a better idea than exotics, with only one or two exceptions.

A SELECTION OF POND PLANTS

FLAG IRIS—IRIS PSEUDACORUS

Of interest to bees for a short time, but mostly good for a pond so that dragonflies have smooth unobstructed leaves to climb up out of a pond.

BULLRUSH LATIN NAME TYPHA

Apart from small flies there isn't much insect interest in this plant. However the stems of the plant are also used for Dragonflies for egg laying and dragonflies emerge by climbing up the stout stems. It grows to 2 metres in height. Buy the smaller **"Typha minima"** for a small pond. Birds such as in the Tit family use the fluffy down to construct nests.

The larger Bullrush have pointed roots that can go through a butyl liner, though not through a solid (fibreglass or moulded) pond. I have a plant of the large Bullrush, and a fibreglass pond on its 12th year. It is possible to control it.

I have read that the larger Bullrush plant was the Middle Ages version of the potato, as the roots were cooked and eaten. I tried this once… But it just tastes like the bottom of a pond, somewhat muddy and not recommended at all.

MINT— MENTHA AQUATICA TYPICAL FLOWERING PERIOD 19/07—01//09

SYMBOLS >>>##**MAX POINTS SCORED 81 INVASIVE SMALL PERENNIAL

All mints are invasive and you can only grow this herb in a tub or a basket in a pond. It grows with horizontal stems across a whole pond in a few years but is easy to cut back.

Watermint is great for hoverflies bees and butterflies but blooms late in my shady garden, it really needs full sun.

Mentha cervina known as Spearmint is a less vigorous choice with the same qualities for insects.

PICKEREL WEED — PONTEDERIA CORDATA

TYPICAL FLOWERING PERIOD 10/07—25/09

SYMBOLS >>* POINTS SCORED 49 SMALL PERENNIAL

One of the most unweed like pond plants, this has purple flowers that are visited by insects including bees. It needs to be planted 10 inches below the surface to survive the Winter but otherwise is trouble free. It is not a UK Native, but will not spread. **Pontedaria lanceolata** or Giant Pickerel weed is also attractive to bees.

MONKEY FLOWER - LATIN NAME - MIMULUS LUTEAUS NOW *ERYTHRANTHE*

GUTTATAS

TYPICAL FLOWERING PERIOD 25/07—30/08

SYMBOLS >>> MAX POINTS SCORED 39 SMALL PERENNIAL

The county flower of Tyne and Wear is a contradictory plant. On the positive side the flowers are good for bees and the plant is undeniably attractive (unless you hate yellow, as someone I used to know did with a passion). But it is a non native invasive and spreading plant to a degree that is making its presence felt in the countryside. It is not as hard to control as the nasties described on previous pages but can still choke a large river area if so minded. It has hybridised and produced a new species In Scotland. So unless plant breeders produce a much less invasive type, I would leave this one alone. HOWEVER **Mimulus luteus** pictured below at Winston Churchills' Chartwell garden and **Mimulus "Orange Glow"** are less invasive, available at Garden Centres and easier to manage whilst still being good for bumblebees.

MARSH MARIGOLD—CALTHA PALUSTRIS

TYPICAL FLOWERING PERIOD 02/03—09/5

SYMBOLS >>>#*~ MAX POINTS SCORED 57 SMALL PERENNIAL

A British native plant and the first pond plant to flower. This attractive plant can flower for 8 weeks or more, and attracts bees and other early emerging insects. It likes mud or can be planted in a basket in the pond where it is well behaved and easy to grow. Very good for wildlife.

WATER PLAINTAIN ALISMA PLANTAGO AQUATICA

TYPICAL FLOWERING PERIOD 25/07—30/08

SYMBOLS ***~~ MAX POINTS SCORED 64 MEDIUM PERENNIAL

One of my favourite native waterside plants which grows in mud or in the water. The flowers are small and dainty and pretty much made for hoverflies or other small insects. Bees are too heavy to balance on the plant to feed from it so hoverflies get a free pass to the nectar.

CHAPTER 11 - GREEN GARDENING - HINTS AND TIPS

In this chapter I look at things you can do you in your garden to both help wildlife and biodiversity, make your garden look better, and in some cases save money.

SOIL THAT HELPS YOUR PLANTS GROW, FOR FREE

I hear an awful lot of complaints where I live about bonfires where people have cut down a bush or a tree in their gardens and burn up the rubbish. For those Councils that offer green waste recycling, there is normally a cost to take away this "rubbish", and a time consuming task to chop up the bits and put them into bags.

There is no need for bonfires 99% of the time. There is no need to send your waste to the Council (or to pay them money). In fact you can save money by making your own compost and the more garden you have, the more compost you can have.

MAKE A SUPER COMPOST HEAP THAT CONVERTS FROM COMPOST TO SOIL IN AS LITTLE AS 8 WEEKS

Imagine you are having a tidying up day in your garden and you are producing a lot of garden "waste".

Firstly if you are cutting down any plants in your garden grade the cuttings into the following types.

TYPE 1 - Soft leafy waste with no stalks (normally perennials or weeds)

TYPE 2 - Woody or soft twigs up to 2mm wide.

TYPE 3 - Woody pieces up to the width of a pencil.

TYPE 4 - Woody pieces that can be easily cut with secateurs.

TYPE 5 - Any branches that need the use of a manual saw or are harder to cut with secateurs.

Putting the Lawn mower over clippings from hedges (Types 1, 2 and 3 as described in this chapter). My battery powered lawnmower works well for this.

Put types 1 and 2 onto the grass. Cut type 3 into short lengths (10—15 centimetres and put them onto the grass. Using a lawn mower with a metal blade (a strimmer is less likely to cope with this scenario) mow the lawn and put the combined grass cuttings and sliced up woody pieces into a pile in a corner. This will heat up in a matter of days (and will need watering in dry weather to keep the process going!) and does not need to be a large heap (even 1 metre high works) to aid a very quick decomposing process. This works because of the combination of some woody material with the grass. This mini compost heap is loved by tiny insects and small flies.

Between April and September the process will be quite quick but you should only distribute when it actually looks like earth. If you see anything green within, it means that plant material has not been killed and you should turn the compost and add some new material. Put a twig into the compost early in the morning and if it is letting off steam (due to the heat of decomposition) then you are on the right track!

The normal rules of composting apply in that you should use material from healthy plants this in particular must apply to Shrubs and Trees. There are some circumstances when burning or disposing of plant material is the only option, such as bacterial diseases (canker for example). And this is the 1% of times that you would need a bonfire (or to dispose of via the Council)

Its worth saying that with my little compost heap I generate the equivalent of up to 10 sacks of compost a year, so that is a saving of about £80 from visiting the garden centre.

MAKE A LOG "STRUCTURE" FOR INSECTS.

You may have noticed no reference above to type 4 and 5 material so far in this chapter. Well I expand on that here.

A log pile is a fantastic way of providing areas for insects and beetles however if you weave together pieces of wood up to 1 metre in length or around the base of an established shrub, it can look a bit better than just a random pile and will have the same effect. If you have a small garden then this can just be a small pile however if you have a larger garden it is possible to make a number of quasi– sculptural piles. Weaving the thinner more supple branches together means you can make a self supporting structure that is narrow and tall, taking up less lateral room. Do this with type 4 and type 5 material. Save stumps and bigger chunks of wood for a "Stumpery" see Chapter 12 for information on how to do this.

MULCHING TO HELP INSECTS AND KEEP DOWN WEEDS, FOR LONGER

I like to term this as "Extreme Mulching" as it is an "outlier" in that it combines a layer of bark, with an under layer of shredded paper or other material. Its a bit radical, but if you have read this far you probably had me figured out that I am.

If you are more artistic than the Author, you can make an attractive sculpture by weaving together thick twigs in a shady corner which will provide beneficial habitat for insects and saving on bonfires as well. After a few years this pile will reduce in height, allowing for more material to be added.

The process of shredded material needs explanation. Whilst some Councils recycle paper, this is a resource that can when carefully used contribute to your garden, shredded paper helps with clay soils to break up the layers and also retains water.

It is also very unattractive to be put directly on the soil, so the premise here is to shred a thick layer of CERTAIN paper material (see table on the next page) and cover that with a thick layer of bark around the plants. Otherwise floaty shreddings of paper are unlikely to impress your neighbour if they blow across to her garden.

I found this mulching prevented any weeds coming back for a year longer than other methods . It also helped the soil be more water retentive. Note that you do need to make certain you remove as many weeds as possible from the area first!

SUITABLE SHREDDING MATERIAL

Firstly, you need a good quality shredder suitable for shredding 11 sheets of paper at a time.

I have used the following successfully having kept a shredder going for 8 years before it eventually broke. The shredder was £25. I obtained £175 of soil from it.

Keep otherwise to paper ONLY. No foil trays. No Christmas Cards with Glitter and nothing which is cloth. Shred carefully as this will be the limit of what a shredder can do. The Author does not accept responsibility for shredding unsuitable items or if you break your shredder.

SHREDDABLE ITEMS

Cardboard Packaging (not thicker than 11 sheets of paper)

"Amazon" style card and paper packing

Printed card food packaging (but not with plastic windows)

Cardboard packing for pet food (but not plastic pouch containers, and no food residue should be shredded)

Old stripped wallpaper . Woven baskets
(where weave is not thicker than 11 sheets)

Wooden food trays (thin slivers of wood only) Old paper lampshades

Paper Bags, some (no glitter) Christmas Cards
Old toilet roll cores

NUTRIENT SOURCE

As part of preparation for this book, I tried using reusable vacuum cleaner bags and then a vacuum that had a plastic container. Provided there is no plastic or food, dust and dander are suitable items to mix with the paper above as this is essentially elements that are already in the air and will break down in time within the soil.

EXTREME MULCHING –THE NEXT STEP

Once you have placed the paper mulch on the area to be treated water it thoroughly to make it into a thick paper "layer" so that the paper does not blow about. Do this by saturating with water and compressing what is there. It is best to collect the shreddings in large bags to stop mess and enable an area to be dealt with.

Then immediately afterwards cover this with a layer of bark from a garden centre. Use any spare type 3 or 4 pieces to supplement that layer afterwards.

EXTREME MULCHING AFTER CARE

The soil structure is affected by this process so do give your plants a little nitrogen fertiliser as paper can temporarily rob nitrogen from the soil. Once done the paper will break down and give nutrients back, though I advocate the same area of soil should not be covered with paper more often than once every 5 years. This does improve the soil condition and is especially good with heavy clay soils. The idea is more suitable for larger gardens because of the need to rotate areas.

MAKE A STUMPERY

A great way of using a shady corner to its best advantage is to plant shade loving (and insect friendly) plants. Logs can be made into sculptural type elements. The combination of this and ferns (which only have the value of providing cover for insects) can make a really magical area. My Stumpery planting plan can be seen in Chapter 12.

FLYING ANT DAY—SUPPORTING, NOT POISONING INSECTS

I get so annoyed when I hear people complaining about "flying ant day", usually a short period of time each Summer when ants reproduce often made reference to as "married" or "nuptial" flight.

Ants have a tough job working for their own community. Then, on the last day of their lives some of them get "married", mate and then die. And you want to kill them, because they get in your hair?

Live and let live, just put up with this natural spectacle which only lasts a day or so. Flying Ants feed bats and birds as they finish their lives. They do good. Change the attitude of others if you can!

BE A LAWN WATCHER, LET IT GROW!

Keep an eye on your lawn and if you see a pile of soil with a hole in it, it could be a bees nest, or fine powdery soil could be an ants nest. Keep clear of this with the lawnmower. And whilst you are about it, why not make a meadow with part of your lawn? This is terrific for all types of insects. But have a plan for this, keep an area unmowed, and you will be amazed at the number of wild flowers that will appear. Consider buying wild flowers to put into the area to make it look even better as described in Chapter 4.

REVIVE A BUMBLEBEE BY BREATHING ON IT

This is safe provided you are careful. If you see a Bumblebee, completely still on a flower, or elsewhere, this may be after a rain shower or when it is not warm and you can help it. Breathe gently on it so that the warmth envelops the bee, and often you will see it recover. Don't continue doing this if it starts flapping its wings. You can think of this as your good deed for the day if the bee is revived enough to fly, to a flower, to feed. Or put a Bumblebee on a flower, if it is on the ground looking slow or unhappy.

USE, RATHER THAN BURN

I had a small wooden bridge in my garden which after 11 years was rotten. I had some other wood from projects in the house including an old garden seat. Rather than burning it, I used the 50% still good wood to make a wooden edging to the border in the garden between plants and grass.

I filled in the gaps in the picture with some pieces of wood from shrubs I had cut down and also used wood from an old garden chair.

After painting this with black woodstain, it made a good edging, and avoided having a bonfire. It is possible to reuse most wood that is not going rotten.

WHAT HAPPENS IN THE FUTURE?

I have already lived in my life the time when parents and myself went out in the car, and the windows were splattered with insects on our journey. Nowadays there are many fewer insects and this does not happen, and it isn't down to car design as some claim. Old cars don't pick up so many insects either. This just reflects the catastrophic decline of insects as a whole in just one lifetime.

Nothing we do as humans seems to consider the creatures we share our planet with. We only need to look at the plastic in the oceans to see that confirmed. And the smaller the creatures the less with think of them. So if we are proposing hundreds of "delivery drones" or "flying taxis" or other technological advancements then think about the consequences! Windfarms kill hundreds of thousands of birds. Drones kill insects. But equally if we had fewer cats, that would save birds. Even well meaning things such as road side wild flower verges are meaningless on the edge of a busy road where insects are killed by the outwash from huge articulated lorries thundering past.

We basically need to think more. In the future we face invasions of insects, birds and other creatures unsuitable for our environment from elsewhere placing our native creatures at risk. From Asian Hornets to Ring Necked Parakeets to Harlequin Ladybirds. Invaders take the space of our struggling native flora and fauna and unbalance nature. And this unbalance is what we will pay a very high price for. We are putting in place this Armageddon of our fellow insects, birds mammals and other creatures without thought on the consequences it will have on the natural world and for us, if we don't find a way to maintain and then increase, biodiversity.

CHAPTER 12 CONCENTRATED ECOLOGY PLANTING

I outlined in chapter 2 the principles behind Ecology Gardening and in subsequent chapters the right plants, with my full research published in the appendixes. This is the final *proper* chapter, so I want to go out with a bang.

PLANTS FOR A WINDOW BOX OR HANGING BASKET

SALVIA "HOT LIPS"   LATIN NAME SALVIA JAMENSIS "HOT LIPS"

TYPICAL FLOWERING PERIOD 20/06—19/08

SYMBOLS >> MAX POINTS SCORED 55 TREATED AS SMALL ANNUAL**

Who can resist hot lips?   I can't resist obtaining this red and white sage. It will only get through one year as it is half hardy but is loved by bees. I have seen it planted in England and Italy and it attracts some bees, everywhere.

However, such options are really expensive in the long run but they are attractive and other Salvias such as **"Blue Note** and **"El Cielo"** are also good for bees. Buy a small plant for a hanging basket as it will spread. A larger plant is a waste of cash.

TICKSEED - LATIN NAME - BIDENS - TYPICAL FLOWERING PERIOD 20/05—15/08 SYMBOLS >>> MAX POINTS SCORED 63 TREATED AS ANNUAL**

Bidens ferulifolia is a half-hardy plant with yellow daisy type flowers. It is liked by most insects and has a trailing habit. Being small it is best at the front of a basket or windowbox. There are larger more trailing plants available and all Bidens are worth trying. One plant already often used in hanging baskets that promotes biodiversity.

HONEYWORT - LATIN NAME - CERINTHE MAJOR

TYPICAL FLOWERING PERIOD —01/07 to 29/08

SYMBOLS >> MAX POINTS SCORED 63 TREATED AS SMALL ANNUAL**

Cerinthe is an unusual looking blue green leaved plant with thick leaves and small tubular flowers.   It is not hardy and is grown as an annual.

BACOPA and TRAILING LOBELIA are often sold as hanging basket plants. These do appeal to hoverflies and in a gentle way to bees . The Lobelia is best of these two however and scores up to 46 points in total with symbols of >>*.

This hanging basket design combines some traditional plants for baskets with **Calamintha,** a small perennial which can be used if it survives the Winter in the following years basket or box.   The blooms otherwise should last from June to September.

If you want this by a back door you could replace **Calamintha** with **single Marigolds** if attracting many insects is bothersome to you.   Otherwise, this basket is attractive to hoverflies and to bees but you will get passing trade, not a crowd.

You can also replace Calamintha with a single trailing **Fuchsia** (often sold for planting in hanging baskets as an alternative. **Poached Egg Plants (Limnanthes douglasii)** can take the place of **Bacopa. Lamium** types can attract early bumblebees. In a window box, there is more soil so you could experiment with small perennials or annuals mentioned in this book. Experimenting with different ideas is fun!

DESIGN FOR A WINDOW BOX OR HANGING BASKET

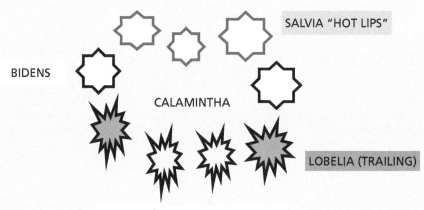

BIDENS

SALVIA "HOT LIPS"

CALAMINTHA

LOBELIA (TRAILING)

BACOPA (WHITE SINGLE TRAILING)

TOP TIP

The key to success is to water the hanging basket every day when it is not raining. The plants in a hanging basket have a limited area of soil so dry out quickly. Buying an already planted basket in late Summer when they are half price can be a good deal as you can plant the basket a new the next year. However hanging basket "kits" are available. The more soil, in the basket, the better for the plants.

A window box can be made from discarded timber or bought as a plastic pot at a garden centre. Incorporate good drainage in the design. Finally be patient, if you are in a city it may take some time for the insects to find your isolated window box. Avoid placing baskets next to a busy road where insects can be killed by traffic

PROJECT 2 THE HOT BED

This really is a design to attract a wide variety of insects from May to October. The scheme starts with the **Ladies Smock**, **Dead-nettle** and **Scabious** combination and finishes with the **Verbena** and **Cosmos**, in bloom until the first frosts.

It positively explodes and fizzes with colour and at different times different plants are more or less dominant. The hot colours make this a very vibrant scheme.

This is a "Concentrated Ecology" plan. So it will look crowded and involves quite a few plants. Earlier blooming plants and bulbs will give way to the others. The plants are mostly not victims of slugs but you must put some grit round the **Cosmos**, and the **Wild Carrot (Daucus carota)** until they start blooming to help them not be eaten. **Cosmos** is an annual plant and the carrot tends to behave like an annual. The **Cistus** is a shrub and the **Penstemon**, where happy will spread and fight for space but you can divide the **Penstemon** easily later on.

Each year, you can review this bed and add or subtract different plants. It makes sense to juggle these elements depending on the plants you like, or those that perform best for you. All these plants are very good for insects. If you have less space you can just plant half of this plan. **Helianthemum (Rock Rose)** will make an alternative, to the **Lamium** and **Calamintha.**

This plan works well in full sun in my garden and on the edge of a wall, and here is a picture of my "hot bed" to prove it! This is 1 metre deep and 2 metres wide.

Left to Right. **Penstemon, Daucus, Cosmos, Allium** and **Calamintha** 17th July.

155

PLANTING PLAN—THE HOT BED

 PENSTEMON—"GARNET"

 CISTUS CORBARIENSIS (ROCK ROSE)

 SCABIOUS "BUTTERFLY BLUE"

 VERBENA BONARIENSES

 COSMOS "CARMINE"

 DAUCUS CAROTA WILD CARROT

 LAMIUM   "PINK CHABLIS "

 HESPERIS MATRONALIS
LADIES SMOCK (WHITE)

 NEPETA MUSSINII "SIX HILLS GIANT"

 KNAUTIA MACEDONICA

 ALLIUM SPHAEROCEPHALON

 CALAMINTHA "BLUE CLOUD"

 LINARIA—PURPLE TOADFLAX

 ALLIUM CRISTOPHII

PROJECT 3—THE STUMPERY—SHADE GARDEN

A complete contrast to Project 2. This is for a garden which gets 4 hours or more of sun at Midsummer but not much in Winter. The use of Logs is beneficial to insects. Dead or dying wood is a great habitat. There are some 900 species of invertebrates that exist and these and other tiny insects help the process of breaking down the wood back into the soil. This plan need some watering in dry weather but the plants featured are quite tough in the main, which they need to be, to survive without much sunlight.

It was the Victorian era in the UK that produced the original "Stumpery" idea, where ferns were interplanted with stumps and a few other shade loving plants. In my plan I go light on the ferns but use some flowering plants that are good for insects and that look like ferns. The **Sorbaria** and **Aruncus** look every bit as beautiful as ferns but do flower at least for a while for the insects.

Foxgloves have been added to the plan. After one year, these *either* need raising from seed by collecting greeny brown seed capsules from this years plants and sow on ordinary compost in a damp shady watered pot *or* require an annual spend to keep the numbers up. The **Welsh Poppy** will seed itself around. The red **Heuchera** is a braver choice here, you can of course choose a green variety for this to be a more "traditional" stumpery. The position of sun is important and the taller plants are on the left, as the plan is South East facing, the most sun occurs to the right, and the front of this bed. Keep the stumps in shadier parts of the area. The plants need the sunniest options. The stumps won't be growing so they don't need sunshine!

 STUMPS / LOGS

 FOXGLOVE VARIETIES

 ARUNCUS DIOEIOUS AND ARUNCUS "HORATIO"

WELSH POPPY - MECONOPSIS CAMBRICA

HEUCHERA VARIETIES MIDNIGHT ROSE / PARIS

FERNS USE—POLYSTICHUM & ASPLENIUM SCOLOPENDRIUM

WALDSTENIA TERNATA

 ANEMONE BLANDA

 GERANIUM MACHRORRIZUM

 SORBARIA "SEM"

Above—Plan of the Stumpery. Below picture of the Stumpery

Geraniums will spread into the shady areas as will the Spring flowering **Waldsteinia ternata.** In early Spring the **Anemone blanda** will gradually spread between the plants, vanishing by May.

Piles of logs can look ugly but a vertical log or stump with branches can look like a brilliant, natural sculpture. As the plants establish, and moss appears the whole thing has the atmosphere of a secret garden. Frogs and Toads will hang out here, eating slugs. Wood wasps (which never harm anyone!) collect slivers of rotten wood to build nests. All types of wasp aid the decomposition of wooden material. If you are lucky solitary bees may nest there, why not drill some 10 centimetre deep pencil sized holes in the stumps. An abandoned, shady, corner can be transformed by making it into a stumpery. At the same time unwanted logs can be made to appear like sculptures within the bed of plants. The size of this bed is 1.5 metres by 2.5 metres.

PROJECT 4—THE HEATHER BED

Heathers are the most valuable early flowering plant for bees. With careful interplanting, the heather bed can deliver even after the flowers have gone by using bulbs and small annual plants. See Chapter 4 for more about heathers. The size of this plan is 1 metre by 2 metres but it can be made larger or smaller by adding or subtracting plants

 LIMNANTHES DOUGLASII—POACHED EGG PLANT

 VARIOUS SPRING FLOWERING HEATHERS IN WHITE PINK AND ROSE (SEE CHAPTER 4 FOR DETAILS)

 PULMONARIA—LUNGWORT (CHAPTER 4 FOR VARIETIES)

 ALLIUM ATROPURPUREUM

 ALLIUM HOLLANDICUM PURPLE SENSATION (PURPLE) AND EVEREST   (WHITE)

 AJUGA FOR VARIETIES SEE CHAPTER 4

The key to success with this plan is to realise the Heathers cannot have plants growing over them or shading them too much as they will tend to sulk if this happens. Fortunately the plants picked here to spend time with the Heather will just go to the edge of the evergreen bushes and can be cut back, if needed, after flowering.

The plan starts its period of interest from February when the Heathers start blooming. The **Pulmonaria** will bloom April until June when the **Alliums** join them. **Allium atropurpureum** is later than **hollandicum** so provides a longer period of interest for the bees. The poached egg plants should self seed and come up in gaps between other plants. The scheme intentionally has an intense period of interest early in the year. The Heathers will then prepare themselves for the next season of flowering, without being shaded over by other plants. This is still 5-6 months of interest and much more forage productive than just heather on its own.

PROJECT 5 - EARLY, MIDDLE AND LATE

This large, perennial, bed will attract pollinating insects right from the early breath of Spring right through to the first frosts of Autumn.

The appearance of **Pulmonaria** in Spring attracts early bees who will also visit the **Lamium. The Oxe Eye, Cirsium, Francoa and Heuchera** take over the Summer shift. Many of the other plants in the plan are exceptionally long flowering and will flower until the first frosts from midSummer. This actually peaks at the end of the season with **Caryopteris, Sunflowers and the Leucanthemella serotina,**

Of course small sections of this can be used in a smaller area as the overall size of this plan is large, 3.5 metres by 1.5 metres.

This is a South or South west facing border—this is important. On the plan, the Sun comes from the top of the page and the shade lovers at the bottom of the page get protection in the Summer when the taller perennials grow up.

PROJECT 5— EARLY MIDDLE AND LATE PLANTING PLAN

 GERANIUM "ROZANNE"

 PULMONARIA

 CARYOPTERIS "WORCESTER GOLD" (Other varieties can be used—see Chapter 5)

 LAVANDULA ANGUSTIFOLIA

 HELIANTHUS "LEMON QUEEN"

 CIRSIUM RIVULARE

 FRANCOA SONCHIFOLIA

 HEUCHERA SILVER SCROLLS

 LEUCANTHENELLA SEROTINA

 OXE EYE DAISY" MAY QUEEN"

 FUCHSIA MAGELLANICA

 PENSTEMON GARNET

 ASTER NOVA BELGII "CRIMSON BEAUTY"

 ASTER FRIKARTII "MöNCH"

PLANTING PLAN—EARLY MIDDLE AND LATE

Left to Right **Aster frikartii "Mönch" Aster Nova-belgii "Crimson Beauty" Helianthus "Lemon Queen" Fuschia magellanica "Riccartonii" and Leucanthenella serotina** Pictured on 5th October.

If you don't want to follow a planting plan, just find some room to select two or three of the recommended plants in the book, even a small addition to your flower bed or even one plant in a pot will help the insects!

APPENDIX -THE STUDY RESULTS OF OVER 520 PLANTS

THANK YOU for reading my book on the subject of insects and plants they need or visit for sustenance in the garden. Writing the book has been a long journey. Over 20 years in planning, 18 months in writing. Here I give you the option to see the conclusion of that journey, full results that produced the selected content you have already read. There are over 520 entries that follow in this list but the book in its entirety covers over 700 individual plants. Almost all were studied and verified for the period of flowering, attractiveness to insects and for negative points in cultivation.

The insects have provided scores for these plants by visiting them, not me! Different areas of the country and the world will have different species of insects and those may favour different plants to mine. This is *my* faithfully reported truth. The scores provide an accurate scale on which to make decisions on wildlife garden planting. There is also a good indication of flowering dates to be able to plan a succession of insect supportive planting. These results are, at the very least, a good contribution to the debate on what we put in our gardens. I think you have to use plants beneficial to insects as your number one gardening rule. Having read this far, do you think there is any point in planting something that does not benefit insects?

There could, in time, be a more detailed study, but it won't include the historical findings going back 20+ years of this book. If there are many fewer insects about in the future it actually won't be possible to undertake a comparable study to this one.

So with the caveat that nothing is perfect, I present you with the results of my study. There is also a series of keys to help interpret the results and provide information about the plants in one handy place. These now follow.

GREEN TINT	RECOMMENDED PLANT
BROWN TINT	SUSCEPTIBLE TO SLUG DAMAGE
ORANGE TINT	NEGATIVE FEATURES SUCH AS POISONOUS / IRRITANT / SPINY / INCLUDING CORROSIVE SAP OR INVASIVE
NO COLOUR	NO NEGATIVES OTHER THAN LESSER SCORE
PINK TINT	DIVA— POTENTIALLY DIFFICULT TO CULTIVATE OR HALF HARDY.
GREY TINT	ZERO SCORE
(N)	NATIVE PLANT
RED AND WHITE	DEADLY TO INSECTS OR PLANT TO AVOID

KEY FOR BEES

>>>> Bees constantly visit the plant which is rarely left unattended during optimum time conditions and sufficient populations. Top scoring plant in my research also taking into consideration preference over other plants

>>> Bees visit the plant with definite and consistent interest during more than 50% of the optimum time and with sufficient populations

>> Bees visit the plant and obtain some benefit but on an irregular, sporadic basis

> Bees rarely visit this plant

KEY FOR BUTTERFLIES (INCLUDING MOTHS WHERE STATED)

Butterflies rarely seen off this plant during optimum times and sufficient populations. The top plants in my research.

Butterflies seen feeding on this plant during optimum times

or # Butterflies have some/little interest in this plant

Also see Chapter 9 for information about Moths relating to this study.

KEY FOR HOVERFLIES

*** Hoverflies favourite plants. Often seen visiting and feeding (and hovering) where there are sufficient populations. The top plants in my study.

** Hoverflies do visit and feed on this plant less than 50% of the optimum time where there are sufficient populations

* Hoverflies visit this plant on a sporadic infrequent basis

KEY FOR OTHER INSECTS - FLIES (including very small flies)
WASPS and others where specifically stated.

~~~ A plant often seen visited by flies and other insects   The top plants in my research

~~ A plant where other insects are found on a regular basis

~ A small but noticeable component is the visiting of other insects

Plant Name Latin	Plant Name English	Comment	Flowering Start	End	Typical Flower period (days)	Codes	Total
Abelia grandiflora	Abelia	Standard Abelia grandiflora is much better than any named cultivars with different colour leaves or flowers	07-Jul	30-Oct	115	>>>>#***~	119
Acanthus	Bears Breeches	Mollis has larger leaves than spinosus. Overall performed poorly. Only large bees could access flowers	20-Jul	20-Aug	31	>>	28
Acer palmatum	Japanese Maple	Many species take some years to flower successfully	20-Apr	30-Apr	10	>>	20
Achillea	Yarrow "Cloth of Gold" and "Terracotta"	Mostly of interest to hoverflies and butterflies	10-Jul	20-Sep	72	***##>>	88
Achillea (also N)	Yarrow other cultivated varieties see article	Mostly of interest to hoverflies and butterflies as is (N) type Achillea millefolium	25-Jun	25-Aug	61	***##>>	85
Aconitum	Monkshood	Skin irritation or severe reaction being a real possibility mean that planting this plant is not recommended.	18-Jun	15-Jul	27	>>	27
Aesculus	Horse Chestnut	Attracts bumblebees	20-Apr	10-May	20	>>>	30
Agapanthus	African Lily	Can be brief in flower and needs attention and Winter mulching to succeed	01-Jul	20-Jul	19	>>>*	40
Agastache	Hyssop	Excellent bee plant but slugs damage plants too easily	10-Jun	20-Jul	40	>>>>##**	90
Ageratum	Floss Flower	Bedding Plant. Annual. Good for bees / butterflies	10-Jul	20-Aug	41	>>##~	60
Agrostemma githago	Corncockle	Annual. Poisonous seeds. Overrated in my opinion as a wildlife plant	04-Jun	01-Aug	58	>>*	45
Ajuga	Bugle plant	See article about various cultivars available including (N) native type	03-May	03-Jun	31	>>*~~	58
Alcea rosea	Hollyhock	Good plant for bees but small plants are very prone to slug damage. Performs best in cracks in pavements. "Rugosa" flowers earlier June to July	20-Jul	10-Sep	52	>>>#*~	73

Alchemilla mollis	Ladies Mantle	Common garden plant	20-Jun	20-Jul	30	~~	28
Alisma plantago-aquatica (N)	Water Plaintain	Pond / Marsh plant, very much liked by Hoverflies	15-Jun	08-Aug	54	***~~	64
Alium	Allium cristophii	Bulb	20-May	10-Jun	21	>>>#**	60
Allium	Allium sphaerocephalon	Bulb	07-Jul	27-Jul	18	>>>>##***	90
Allium	Purple Sensation	The best of the Alliums	07-May	25-May	18	>>>>##***	90
Allium	Chives	Mainly will flower in June	01-Jun	20-Jun	19	>>>##**	70
Alliaria petiolata (N)	Garlic Mustard	Fairly attractive wild flower, good for hoverflies. Food plant for orange tip butterfly	10-Apr	30-Apr	20	>**~##	60
Allium ursinum	Ramsons (N)	Invasive native Onion	20-Apr	30-Apr	10	>~	20
Alnus	Alder (N)	Pollen only	03-Mar	16-Mar	13	>	10
Alstroemeria	Peruvian Lily	Tricky plants subject to slug damage also.	10-Jun	05-Sept	87	>>>*	62
Amelanchier lamarckii	Snowy Mespil	Also has berries for birds	25-Apr	14-May	19	>>	20
Anaphalis	Pearl Everlasting		01-Jul	01-Aug	31		0
Anchusa	Anchusa	Blue flowered, sunny position, dry soil	30-Apr	20-Jun	51	>>>	43
Anemone blanda	Windflower	Useful early plant	25-Mar	20-Apr	26	>>>	37
Anemone	Anemone de Caen	Only sporadic attention from bees	10-Apr	25-Apr	15	>>	20
Anemone hybrida	Anemone	Autumn flowering daisies, have never had huge success despite in theory being good plant	20-Aug	20-Sep	31	>>**	48
Anethum	Dill	Fennel is a better plant	01-Jun	10-Jul	39	**	30
Angelica	"Archangelica"	Angelica gigas is TOO attractive to wasps. Angelica archangelica is a good and relatively early plant for wildlife but prone to slug damage - results for that included here	30-Apr	30-May	30	>>##~	58

Anthemis	Feverfew	"EC Buxton" is an ok plant for hoverflies but slug damage is a certainty, so plant in gravel, which may avoid the problem	20-Jun	20-Jul	30	**>	38
Anthemis	Chamomile	Liked by Ladybirds	20-Jul	20-Sep	62	~	26
Antirrhinum	Snapdragon	Annual. Results vary, the best plants are the strongest growing in various colours though for me, the red plants attracted most bumblebees.	07-Jul	20-Sep	75	>>	39
Anthriscus sylvestris (N)	Cow Parsley	A wild flower of wooded path edges, this is only ok for flies and early hover flies	15-Apr	15-May	30	#~	28
Apple	Malus species	Attract all types of bee including solitary bees	20-Apr	15-May	25	>>>	36
Aquilegia	Ladies Bonnets	Avoid doubles such as "Nora Barlow" though improved varieties such as "Georgia" are good for bees. See article	03-May	14-Jun	42	>>>*~	61
Arabis	Rock Cress	Rock garden plant which is useful for some early insects	20-Apr	15-May	25	>>*	36
Aralia	Japanese Angelica Tree	Very spiny tree but in its variegated form provides a useful supply of pollen and nectar for late bees	20-Aug	10-Oct	51	>>>*	53
Arbutus unedo	Strawberry Tree	Native to West Ireland	25-Sep	20-Oct	25	>>>	36
Argyranthemum	Jamaican Primrose	A one year deal this, good for hoverflies	20-Jun	20-Aug	61	>>***	65
Argyranthemum	Chrysanthemum	A large genus. Autumn "Garden mums" as they are known bloom very late and are often offered as double varieties. Single varieties are very good for insect life but many bloom so late there will not be many visitors	10-Sep	25-Oct	30	>>**	51
Argyranthemum	Chrysanthemum	Rock plant "Weyrichii"	21-Jun	01-Aug	41	>>>	40
Armeria	Thrift	Wild (N) native flower found on cliff tops	30-Apr	30-Jun	61	>>	35
Arnica montana	Wolfs Bane	Yellow Daisy native to Mountains in Europe	01-May	01-Aug	61	>>*	45
Arona	Chokeberry		25-May	10-Jun	16	>>	20
Artemisia lactifolia	Mugwort	Not visited by insects	20-Sep	20-Oct	30		0

Arum maculatum	Lords and Ladies (N)	Wild flower which is attractive to flies in Spring	15-May	01-Jun	17		~~	20
Aruncus	Goatsbeard	See article on different types of plant	02-Jul	20-Jul	18		>>>**	50
Asclepias	Butterflyweed	Has milky sap which is poisonous. Avoid Asclepias syriaca (Invasive) It is said to make bees drunk on the nectar though there is no information on whether this is harmful or not as yet!	20-Jul	21-Sep	63		>>>*##	76
Asphodeline lutea	Kings Spear	Good bee plant of untidy habit	30-May	30-Jun	31		>>>	38
Aster frikartii	Michaelmas Daisy "Mönch"	The best of the "frikartii" types which all start to flower by August	27-Jul	10-Oct	75		>>>##***~	109
Aster Novae Angliae	Michaelmas Daisies	See main article. Score is for "Alma Pötchke" and "Little Pink Beauty"	01-Sep	30-Oct	59		>>>**	65
Astilbe	Astilbe	Much as I like the colour of the plant, Astilbes hold little to no interest for any insects	20-Jun	20-Jul	30			
Astrantia	Astrantia	I love this plant for wildlife but slugs like it too	06-Jun	06-Jul	30		>>>#~*	68
Aubrietia	Aubretia	Keep with old varieties only	01-Mar	30-Apr	60		>>~~	55
Aucuba japonica	Laurel	Laurel bushes discharge cyanide from leaves and can kill insects	20-Apr	15-May	25		>>	26
Aurinia saxitile	Allysum		10-Apr	09-May	29	>*		27
Azara microphylla	Azara	Hardy to -10 celcius	10-Apr	15-May	35		>>	29
Azalea	Azalea	See plants to avoid section	20-Apr	15-May	25		>>>	36
Baptisia	False Indigo	Bees have to work out the flower. Plant does not like lime in the soil	04-Jun	01-Jul	27		>>	27
Bellis perennis (N)	Daisy	Small insects only.	20-Apr	20-Jul	91		~	33

Berberis	Berberis	Stenophylla. Prickly beast	01-Jun	20-Jun	19		>>>	30
Bergenia	Elephants Ears	Sporadic, sometimes favoured	20-Jan	15-Mar	54		>>	34
Ballota	Horehound	See entry on Horehound	10-Jun	20-Aug	71		>>>**	68
Bacopa	Water Hyssop		20-Jun	20-Aug	61		>*	35
Bidens	Tickseed	Often used in Council hanging baskets. Good for insects.	01-Jul	01-Oct	92	>>**		63
Blackstonia perfoliata	Yellow Wort	Wild flower, yellow	01-Jun	01-Jul	30	>		18
Boltonia	False Aster	An alternative to Michaelmas Daisies. Can be very tall to over 1.5 metres. Rarely found but try Asteroides Needs moist soil.	19-Aug	25-Sep	37	>>>*#		59
Borage	Borage	Coarse and rough annual that is very attractive to the bees. For a wild corner this is great	15-Jun	05-Aug	51	>>>>*~		73
Brachyglottis	var "Sunshine"	Ubiquitous plant on verges and in gardens that flowers briefly	15-Jul	26-Jul	11	>>**		40
Brachyscome	Swan River Diasy	Annual, but there are better choices.	10-Jul	10-Aug	31	>~*		38
Brunnera macrophylla	Heartleaf Brunnera	"Hadspen Cream"and "Jack Frost" have forget-me -not like flowers.	30-Apr	30-May	30	>>		28
Buddleia davidii	Buddleia	See main article. Score relates to maximum possible attainable	30-Jun	10-Sep	72	>>>>***####~		138
Buddleia alternifolia	Buddleia Small Leaved	Not as good as Davidii for insects	14-Jun	01-Jul	17	>>>**##		70
Buddleia davidii	"White profusion" variety	Said to be especially attractive to moths	20-Jul	10-Sep	52	>>>***###		103
Buddleia weyeriana "Sungold"	Buddleia Variety	See main article	03-Jun	10-Aug	68	>>>**~##		97

Buphthalmum salicifolium	Yellow Ox-Eye	Closely related to Telekia/ Inula this is a good earlier daisy in the garden. Needs sun/well drained soil but is very hardy	20-May	20-Aug	92	>>>**	73
Bupleurum fruticosum	Hares Ear	An evergreen "Subshrub" and quite large (Up to 2 metres) A very good bee plant but needs everything hot, well drained, sunny. Acid yellow umbels of flowers	30-Jun	30-Aug	61	>>>**	65
Butomus umbellatus (N)	Flowering Rush	Often planted in ponds	20-Jun	20-Jul	30	>*	28
Calamintha	Calamint	Calamintha "Nepeta" is One of the very best wildlife plants, not trumpeted in many other books. Ideal growing over a wall in full sunshine.	01-Jul	20-Sep	81	>>>>***###~~	150
Calendula	Marigold	Single flowered (annual) orange marigolds are often used in bedding, they have greater value than many other bedding plants	01-Jul	30-Oct	121	>>>***~	100
Calicarpa	Beauty bush	Not sure the berry is that attractive to anything?	01-Aug	10-Aug	10	>**	30
Callistemon	Bottlebrush	Protect from frost. Only water with rain water, grow in a pot in hard water (alkaline) areas	20-May	30-Jun	41	>>>>**	70
Caltha palustris (N)	Marsh Marigold	Early pond plant and if the bees are about, they will visit	02-Mar	09-May	68	>>>*-	57
Calystegia sepium	Bindweed (N)	The wild plant is a pernicious weed which you don't want taking over your borders.	01-Jul	01-Aug	50	>	23
Camassia leichtlinii	Quamash	Much disappointment in this floppy bulb. Try Alliums !	01-May	25-May	24	>>	26
Camelia	Camelia	Single varieties bloom in mid to late Winter, but bees favour other plants when about	01-Jan	28-Feb	58	>	25
Campanula "Loddon Anna"	Harebell	Other Campanula plants are better for insects	10-Jun	20-Aug	71	>	28

Campanula poscharskyana	Harebell	This form is a very vigorous plant which likes cracks in pavements. It does need controlling but is a good bee plant when it is out	10-Jun	15-Jul	35	>>>*	49
Campanula takesiwana	Campanula	Variety "Elizabeth" is loved by bees. Unusual grey pink flower	10-Jun	05-Jul	25	>>>	36
Campsis	Trumpet Vine	Annual climber in UK. Mixed results. Grows 2 metres plus in a year!	20-Jul	30-Aug	41	>>	30
Cardamine pratensis (N)	Cuckoo Flower	Food plant of orange tip butterfly. Wet marshy places	12-Apr	10-May	28	>##~	47
Carpenteria californica	Tree Anenome	Rarely cultivated shrub with big potential	01-Jul	06-Aug	36	>>**	49
Caryopteris clandonensis	Bluebeard	See article about various cultivars available	23-Aug	20-Sep	28	>>>>***###~	117
Caryopteris incana	Bluebeard	See article	01-Sep	15-Oct	44	>>>>***###~	121
Castanea sativa	Sweet Chestnut	Large tree. European Native. Good for pollinating insects	20-Jun	10-Jul	20	>>>**	50
Centaurea argentea	Cornflower	Silver foliage and full sun well drained soil	01-Jul	02-Aug	32	>	10
Centaurea macrocephala	Cornflower	Large coneflower which is good for bees and butterflies	20-Jul	20-Aug	31	>>>##**~	88
Centaurea montana	Knapweed	Blue ground cover plant with short flowering period. A similar plant is "John Coutts" which is a rose coloured flower	12-Jun	04-Jul	22	>>#**	56
Centaurea nigra (N)	Wild Knapweed	Native Meadowflower	29-May	05-Aug	68	>>>####**	107
Centranthus	Valerian	Good plant for butterflies moths and bees but too invasive. If you do grow it, cut all flowers off before it goes to seed. Can cause damage to walls and pavements	20-May	20-Sep	123	>>>**###	111
Ceanothos	Californian Lilac	Evergreen species vary. The best variety I found was Ceanothus thyrsiflorus "Skylark"	09-May	31-May	22	>>>#	46

Ceanothos	Gloire De Versailles	Large shrub, which has a very late flowering spike sometimes as late as Christmas	01-Jul	20-Sep	81	>>>***~	95
Cephalaria gigantea	Giant Scabious	A large and unruly plant whose flowers may droop and flop but like other scabious is a brilliant insect plant and well worth the effort. Over 2 metres	20-Jun	01-Aug	42	>>>>###***~	121
Ceratostigma	Shrubby Plumbago	Needs sunny sheltered position	01-Aug	01-Nov	92	**#	53
Cercis siliquastrum	Judas Tree	Attracts bees	15-May	30-May	15	>>	20
Cerinthe major	Honeywort	Annual very attractive to bees	01-Jul	29-Aug	59	>>**	63
Chaerophyllum	Chervil (N)	Attractive for a short time to insects	01-Jun	01-Jul	30	>>	28
Chamaenerion	Rosebay Willowherb	The white variety is recommended. The pink plant of hedgerows is too rampant and should not be planted in gardens	25-Jul	10-Sep	47	>>>#**	72
Cheiranthus cheiri	Wallflowers	Biennial Wall flower	15-Mar	20-May	66	>>*#	57
Chelone	Turtlehead	Bumblebees have to work out the way in and often don't	02-Jun	25-Jun	23	>	16
Chimonanthus	Wintersweet	For Winter Bumblebees only	01-Jan	01-Feb	31	>>	28
Choisya	Choisya	"Sundance" & "Aztec Pearl" flower sporadically, they don't have a good flower/ space ratio	24-May	14-Jun	21	>>	20
Chrysanthemum Segetum	Corn Marigold	Contains natural insecticide properties which causes concern but liked by pollinating insects. Rare naturalised plant in the UK	01-Jun	20-Aug	80	>>*#	60
Chrysogonum	Golden Star	Flowers for 4 months if you can find one. Rarely found	01-May	01-Aug	92	>>	43
Cichorium intybus	Chicory	Untidy plant but very good for bees. Flowers only open for part of the day.	01-Jul	01-Aug	31	>>>**	58
Cimicifuga racemosa	Bugbane	Can have an unpleasant smell but has interest from insects	20-Aug	10-Oct	53	>>>**##	83

Circaea lutetiana(N)	Enchanters Nightshade	A pernicious weed of some use to hoverflies but you will fight battles to be rid of it.	15-Jun	25-Aug	71	>*	38
Cirsium palustre	Thistle	Invasive native thistle, the weed type, not the garden type, though insects love it	20-Jun	22-Jul	32	>>>**#	68
Cirsium rivulare	Plume Thistle. Atropurpereum	Very good bee plant. See article	01-May	10-Jun	40	>>>**	60
Cirsium tuberosm	Thistle	Cultivated thistle type	23-Jun	25-Aug	63	>>>**#	76
Cistus corbariensis	Rock Rose	See article about various cultivars available	15-May	20-Jun	36	>>>>***##	99
Clematis heracleifolia	Perennial Clematis	Clematis elicit little response	09-Jun	10-Jul	31	>	18
Clematis montana	Clematis	Not any good in my experience and grows too quickly as my neighbour is finding out!	01-Apr	01-May	30	~	18
Clematis vitalba	Travellers Joy (N)	Not for gardens, an invasive climber best left in the wild. Food plant for Chalk Carpet, Small Emerald and Small Waved Umber Moths	22-Apr	19-May	50	>>*##	57
Cleome	Spider flower	Annual spikey plant and can cause skin inflammation. Good plant for insects otherwise	01-Jul	01-Aug	31	>>**#	58
Clerodendron	Harlequin Glorybower	Clerodendrum trichotomum var. fargesii is a shrub with bee attractive flowers and metallic blue berries.	01-Jul	01-Aug	31	>>	28
Clethra	Sweet Pepper Bush	Shrub prefers slightly acidic conditions, widely reported as a good, late bee and butterfly plant. Clethra alnifolia "Hummingbird" is white "Ruby Spice" pink	15-Aug	25-Sep	41	>>>*#-	60
Colchicum	Autumn Crocus	Seems to flop before visited by anything!!	01-Sep	01-Oct	30	>>	28
Colutea	Bladder Senna	An early flowering shrub with some climbing tendancies. Great for early bumblebees	28-Mar	20-May	53	>>>*~	63
Conopodium majus	Pignut (N)		01-Jun	15-Jun	14	>>	20

Convallaria (N)	Lily of the Valley	Brief blooming. Poisonous	01-May	01-Jun	31	>	18
Convolvulus cneorum	Convolvulus Bush	Short flowering period, should be of interest to hoverflies. I think it is a waste of space!!	10-Jun	25-Jun	15	**	20
Coreopsis	Tickseed	"Flying Saucers" "Moonbeam" "Zagreb" "Tripteris" "Rosea" and other single varieties are brilliant pollinator plants but will be subject to slug damage	01-Jul	01-Oct	92	>>>***##	103
Cornus	Dogwood	Flowers are brief	01-Jun	01-Jul	30	>	18
Cornus controversa	Wedding Cake Tree	Variety "Variegata" an impressive small tree loved by bees and early hoverflies but takes many years to establish	04-May	29-May	25	>>>**	56
Corydalis	Corydalis	Seen in blue and yellow forms	01-Jun	01-Jul	30	>	18
Corylopsis glabrescens	Winter Hazel	Shrub. Needs acidic soil, does little the rest of the year	01-Mar	01-Apr	31	>>	28
Cosmos	Cosmos	See article	05-Jun	10-Oct	127	>>>>##***~	132
Cotinus	Smoke bush	Not even a fly. Why?	01-Jul	01-Aug	31		0
Cotoneaster	Cotoneaster horizontalis	Fantastic for 2 minutes	15-May	01-Jun	17	>>>>#*	60
Cotoneaster watereri	Tree Cotoneaster	See article	05-Jun	30-Jun	25	>>>>**#~~	96
Crambe cordifolia	Kale	Why you should want to plant something that smells this bad?	03-Jul	17-Jul	14	~~~	30
Crataegus monogyna	Hawthorn (N)	Double forms attract nothing	04-May	06-Jun	33	>>#*~	58
Crataegus crus-galli	Hawthorn	More spikey than the hawthorn above. Berries too big for birds?	10-Jun	20-Jun	10	>>>	30
Crepis	Dandelion (N)	A wild flower that blooms early and is great for bees.	01-Apr	15-May	61	>>>*#	61
Crinodendron	Chilean Lantern Tree	Moderately hardy	01-Aug	01-Sep	31	>>	28

Crocosmia	Crocosmia "Lucifer"	See article	10-Jul	11-Aug	32	>>~~	48
Crocus	Crocus Mixed	See article	25-Feb	31-Mar	34	>>>*	49
Cyclamen	Cyclamen		15-Sep	15-Oct	50	>	23
Cynara scolomus	Globe Artichoke	Very attractive to bees. Needs sunshine and well drained soil	01-Jul	01-Sep	62	>>>##	66
Cynoglossum	Hounds Tongue	Like a darker blue forget me not	15-Apr	15-May	30	>	18
Cytisus	Broom	Sporadic periods of great attraction to bees followed by no interest at all	07-Apr	09-May	32	>>>	38
Dactylorhiza fuchsii	Orchid	Attractive to bees but rarely found in garden centres / can be tricky	09-Jun	10-Jul	31	>>	28
Dahlia	Dahlia	See article, very good for insects	01-Jul	10-Oct	100	>>>***#	95
Daphne laureola (N)	Spurge Laurel	Poisonous berries. Visited by a few early bees	18-Feb	01-Mar	11	>	10
Darmera peltata	Umbrella Plant		15-Apr	01-May	16	>	10
Datura species	Thorn Apple	Unpleasant smell Poisonous seeds. Can kill bees and most likely is bad for other insects.	01-Jul	01-Aug	31	>	18
Daucus carota (N)	Wild Carrot	One of the best native plants for the "other" insects Food plant of Yellow Belle Moth	17-Jun	18-Aug	62	~~~***	76
Delphinium	Delphinium	These plants offer little to insects	15-Jun	10-Aug	56		0
Dendranthema	Previously Chrysanthemum	It is very late into flower so does rely on insects being actually out themselves	10-Sep	01-Nov	52	>>	33
Dendranthema weyrichii	Previously Chrysanthemum	Rockery plant and liked by bees and hoverflies	25-Jul	18-Aug	24	>>>**	58
Deutzia elegantissima	Deutzia	Very short flowering dull shrub	15-Jun	01-Jul	16	>>*	30
Dianthus	Carnation	Not attractive to anything except an antiquated button hole	02-Jun	10-Aug	69		0
Diascia	Twinspur	Bees do visit some types of this tender perennial	10-Jun	22-Aug	73	>>	38

Dicentra	Lady in a Bath	Bleeding Heart aka Lamprocapnos spectabilis	01-Apr	01-May	30	>>	22
Dictamnus	Burning Bush	Pollinated by a few bees	01-Jul	01-Aug	31	>	18
Digitalis	Foxglove	See article on different varieties	19-May	05-Jul	47	>>>> *	62
Dipsacus	Teasel	A wild, wild prickly biennial that can self seed a lot... you can either dead head, or pull up many unwanted plants	10-Jul	30-Aug	51	>>>**##	73
Dorinicum	Leopards Bane	Good early plant with only negative of not always coming back the next year...	25-Mar	25-Apr	31	>>***	58
Dracocephalum	Dragons Head	Rarely found relative of Catmint - try "Blue Dragon"	15-Jun	01-Aug	47	>>>*	52
Dryas octopetala (N)	Mountain Avens	Plant of mountains and the north of the UK . Good for bees. It is Icelands national flower needs very cool conditions and occurs naturally in the North and Far North	20-Jun	15-Jul	25	>>>**	56
Eccremocarpus scaber	Chilean Glory Flower	Annual Climber	01-Jul	01-Sep	62	~	26
Echinacea	Cone Flower	Bumblebees love this plant	14-Jul	09-Sep	57	>>>*#	64
Echinops	Globe Thistle	All varieties of this are attractive to insects	10-Jun	20-Jul	40	>>>##**	80
Echium pininana	Tower of Jewels	The tall plant found in Cornish Gardens. Lives 2-3 years. Not hardy. Sometimes found in garden centres, if you have time, and seek relevant advice, one of the best bee plants	15-Jun	20-Aug	56	>>>>*#	73
Echium vulgare (N)	Vipers Bugloss	Native Bugloss is one of the best of our wild flowers for pollinating insects	16-Jun	20-Aug	65	>>>>##*~	96
Elaeagnus	Elaeagnus	Evergreen shrub which is not visited by my bees	01-Jul	15-Jul	14	~	10
Elsholtzia	Elsholtzia	Blue sub shrub with minty leaves	01-Jul	01-Aug	31	>>	28
Epimedium	Bishops Hat	Early pollinators will visit	01-Apr	01-May	30	>>*~	48

Eranthis	Winter aconite	Where I am, Crocus is preferred	01-Mar	20-Mar	19	>>	20
Eremurus	Foxtail Lily	I thought this would be fabulous for bees when I grew it but it wasn't and it can be tricky to grow	10-Jun	10-Jul	30	>>	28
Erica	Irish Heath	See article, best early plant	20-Jan	25-Apr	95	>>>>**~	94
Calluna	Heather	Late Summer flowering Heather needs acid soil	20-Aug	20-Sep	31	>>>>~	58
Erigeron	Fleabane	Cultivated types should be Slugbane on my experience.	01-Jun	01-Jul	30	>*	28
Eriophyllum lanatum	Woolly Sunflower	Good for pollinators, native of hot sunny California. Better choices	01-Jul	01-Aug	31	>#*	38
Erysimum	Perennial Wallflower	"Bowles Mauve" Flowering decreases from mid August	20-Mar	16-Aug	149	>>>**###	117
Erodium	Storks Bill	Carvofoliium is much grown it is ok for bees but not as good as geraniums. Plant is good in dry gardens and full sun	01-Jul	01-Aug	31	>>**	48
Eryngium	Sea Holly	Alpinum / Bourgattii are good. I have grown Tripartitum which is loved by bees and hoverflies	01-Jul	01-Aug	31	>>>##***	98
Erythronium	Dog tooth Lily	Likes acid soil	01-Apr	01-May	30	>	18
Escallonia	Escallonia	Good evergreen hedge attractive short lived blooms for pollinators	14-Jun	28-Jun	14	>>**	40
Escholtzia	Californian Poppies	The orange plants are more vigorous and flower for a longer time than other colours	01-Jul	30-Aug	60	>>*~~	65
Eucryphia x nymansensis	Eucryphia	See article.	23-Aug	16-Sep	24	>>>>**#~	86
Euonymus alatus	Spindle Tree	Hoverflies. Birds like berries	25-May	05-Jun	11	**~	30
Eupatorium	Agrimony	Hemp or Joe Pye Weed. Prone to slugs	21-Aug	20-Sep	30	>>>###~	78

Euphorbia	Spurge	All plants contain milky poisonous sap which is an irritant to skin. Plants are of some use to insects but not exceptional on the whole	01-May	01-Jul	61	>>	35
Euphorbia cyparissias	Euphorbia	It is considered a wild flower but I didn't see insects much	30-Apr	30-May	30	~	18
Euphrasia Sp	Eyebright	Pollinated by a few bees	01-Jun	01-Jul	30	>>	28
Euryops	Yellow Daisy Bush	Euryops pectinatus needs excellent soil drainage and full sun. Small Shrub	01-Jul	15-Sep	76	>>**#~	79
Exochorda x macrantha	Bridal Wreath	Brief blooming shrub	15-May	09-Jun	25	~>	16
Fatshedia	X Ivy & Fatsia	Has sticky nectar	09-Sep	09-Oct	30	>~~	38
Fatsia japonica	Cheese Plant		01-Sep	01-Oct	30	>#~	38
Ferula vulgaris	Fennel	Bronze is as good as the green variety for hoverflies, this is a great favourite for them and also for small flies	01-Aug	10-Sep	40	***~~~	70
Ferula communis	Fennel (Giant)	For the dry garden but also needs Winter protection	01-Jun	01-Sep	92	>>>***	83
Filipendula rubra	Meadowsweet	Often sold as good for bees this plant (N) is an adequate plant overall but with a short flowering period "Venusta" is pretty. Keep this damp at all times	20-Jun	10-Jul	20	>>##~	50
Forsythia	Forsythia	Big Fat Zero	28-Feb	20-Mar	20		0
Fothergilla	Witch Alder	Reports elsewhere state this is more bee friendly than my results concluded	20-Apr	05-May	15	>>	20
Fragaria vesca (N)	Strawberry	Wild strawberry brief nectar for insects	20-Apr	20-May	30	>	23
Francoa sonchifolia	Bridal Wreath	See article	20-Jun	10-Aug	51	>>>***###~~~	133
Fremontodendron	California Glory	Skin Irritant. Native to S. USA not "happy" in UK	01-Jul	01-Aug	31	>~	28
Fritillaria imperialis	Crown Imperial	Grand early blooming plant plant bulb 15cms deep	01-Apr	01-May	30	>>	28
Fritillaria meleagris (N)	Snakes Head Frittilary	The one off Spring flower	22-Apr	05-May	13	>>>	30

Fuchsia magellanica	Fuschia	This is the hardy form seen on roadsides in Ireland. A beautiful plant that flowers until the first frosts. See article	05-Jul	10-Oct	97	>>>~~~	84
Fuchsia riccartonii	Fuschia	Smaller than Fuchsia magellanica and better for a small garden	20-Jul	01-Oct	73	>>>~~~	78
Gaillardia	Blanket Flower	See article	25-Jul	10-Sep	47	>>>**	62
Galanthus (N)	Snowdrops	Often too early for bees	01-Feb	18-Feb	17	>	10
Galega orientalis	Goats Rue	Does attract bees. Flops. Isn't so great in a small garden	01-Jul	30-Jul	29	>>	27
Galium aparine (N)	Goose Grass	Sticky weed.	10-Apr	30-Apr	20	~	10
Gallium verum (N)	Ladies Bedstraw	Meadow plant and perennial. Food plant of the Elephant Hawk Moth, Gallum Carpet Moth, Plain /Riband Wave Moth, Bedstraw Hawk Moth, Oblique Striped Moth, Stripped Hawk-moth, Archer's Dart, Red Chestnut Moth and Hummingbird Hawk-moth	20-Jul	15-Aug	26	>>***###~~	107
Galtonia		Bulb that does attract bees but all Alliums are much better than this	01-Jul	01-Aug	31	>>	28
Gaura lindheimeri		Not a foolproof hardy plant, liked by hoverflies. "The Bride" is good	01-Jul	01-Oct	92	~**	53
Gazania		Is visited by bees but single flower types only	02-Jul	20-Aug	49	>>	32
Gentian		9 cm high blue flowers	11-Feb	22-Mar	39	>>	30
Geranium	Geranium "Ann Folkard" Rose Pink		01-Jul	01-Aug	31	>>>*	48
Geranium	Geranium Rozanne	Blue Variety	20-Jun	20-Sep	92	>>>>#**~	103
Geranium	Geranium Patricia	See article for other geraniums	15-Jun	20-Jul	35	>>>**	59
Geranium robertianum (N)	Herb Robert	A weed, Innocent little flowers are good for small insects	20-Apr	20-May	30	>~	28
Geranium pratense (N)	Meadow Cranes Bill	See article	20-Jun	20-Jul	30	>>>**	58

Geum	Avens	See article	15-May	15-Jun	31	>>**	48
Gilia	Queen Annes Thumb	California Native, is attractive more to bees in USA	01-Jul	01-Aug	31	>	18
Glaucium flavum	Horned Poppy	For a dry, gravel garden this is a great plant and various insects favour it (N)	13-Jul	10-Aug	28	>>**~	57
Glechoma hederacea (N)	Ground Ivy		30-Mar	17-Apr	18	>>	20
Gleditsia triacanthos	Honey Locust	Tree struggles to flower in UK	05-Jun	05-Jul	30	>	18
Gunnera manicata	Gunnera	Far too large for most gardens. Pollinating from flies	02-Jul	10-Jul	8	~	10
Gypsophila paniculata	Baby's Breath		10-Jul	02-Aug	23	>	16
Halesia monticola	Snowball Tree		20-May	10-Jun	21	>>>	30
Halimiocistus		Small early ish flowering shrub liked by hoverflies and bees but may not make it through the Winter unless very sheltered	01-Apr	01-May	30	>>*	38
Hamamelis	Witch Hazel		01-Jan	30-Jan	29	>	17
Hebe	Hebe "MidSummer Beauty"	One of the very best plants for insects. This also has a significant second flowering period between August and October	20-Jun	20-Jul	30	>>>>>###***~~	128
Hebe rakaiensis	Hebe	There are better Hebes than this though for a period of a few days this is very interesting to insects	20-Jun	10-Jul	20	>>>###~~	80
Hedera helix (N)	Ivy	See article. important for the Ivy Bee Colletes hederae	01-Sep	01-Nov	61	>>>#*	65
Helenium	Sneezeweed	A great bee plant but also is a favourite for a slugs breakfast. See article	25-Jul	20-Aug	26	>>>>***####	117
Helianthemum	Rock Rose	See article, the wild (N) plant is the food plant of the Brown Argus, Green Hairstreak and Silver Studded Blue Butterfly	01-May	15-Jun	45	>>>***	71
Helianthus	Sunflower	See article	01-Jul	10-Sep	43	>>>**	61

Helianthus	Sunflower (Perennial)	See article on "Lemon Queen"	20-Jul	15-Oct	97	>>>>***###	124
Helichrysum italicum	Curry Plant	Smells of curry, Insects are not, clearly, well disposed towards curry	10-Jun	15-Jul	35	>	19
Heliopsis	False Sunflower	Helianthoides "Light of Loddon" is the best choice Very good bee & other insect plants. Utterly decimated by slugs always	05-Jul	15-Sep	72	>>>**~	78
Helleborus foetidus (N)		Hellebore	30-Dec	30-Mar	90	~<	33
Hellebore niger	Christmas Rose	Niger and Orientalis	30-Dec	18-Apr	109	>>~	57
Hemerocallis	Day Lily	"Corky" and "Harlequin" are recommended, but not as good as other plants for bees out at this time.	01-Jul	10-Aug	40	>>*	40
Hesperis matronalis (N)	Ladies Smock	Food plant orange tip butterfly	20-Apr	20-Jun	61	>>####**	95
Heuchera	Coral Bells	Flowers are unassuming but a very good bee plant which can flower later than shown. See article	01-Jun	14-Aug	74	>>>**~	79
Hibiscus	Hibiscus	Despite appearances that suggest a good bee plant, it simply isn't	01-Sep	01-Oct	30	>	18
Hieracium	Fox and Cubs	Cultivated form of (orange) Hawkweed and sold as a wildlife friendly plant. Does not flower for very long or do much for insects. Avoid.	01-May	01-Jun	31	~>	28
Hippocrepis comosa	Horseshoe Vetch	Chalkhill blue Adonis blue butterfly flood plant (N)	15-Jun	10-Jul	25	>>	26
Hoheria angustifolia	Narrow Leaved Laceback	Evergreen tree with white flowers	01-Jun	16-Jun	15	>~#	30
Holodiscus discolor	Oceanspray	Very similar to Sorbaria, but a more pleasant smell!	17-Jun	20-Jul	33	>>~~##	68
Hosta	Plaintain Lily	Many hostas are grown only for foliage (and slugs) those that are flowering, are attractive to bees but those varieties are short flowering, unfortunately	01-Jul	01-Aug	31	>	18

Humulus	Hop	These plants are pollinated by honey bees.	07-Jul	10-Aug	34	>>>	39
Hyacinthus orientalis	Common Hyacinth		01-Mar	01-Apr	31	>	18
Hyacinthoides non-scripta	Bluebells	If planted only plant UK Bluebells due to the interaction with the Spanish Bluebell in the wild.	18-Apr	14-May	26	>>>	37
Hydrangea arborescens	Hydrangea	USA native "original" Hydrangea. The only way to buy an insect friendly Hydrangea is by observation at a garden centre. 95% of varieties offer nothing to insects	20-Jul	15-Aug	26	>>>*	47
Hydrangea macrophylla	Mop Head Hydrangea		25-Jul	25-Aug	30		
Hypericum	St Johns Wort (N)	See article	01-Jul	10-Aug	40	>>*	40
Iberis	Candytuft	White flowered perennial	05-Apr	20-May	45	>>	31
Ilex	Holly (N)	Inconspicious flowers, pollinated by bees	25-Apr	16-May	21	>>>	30
Indigofera	Indigofera	Is attractive to bees in May and June but is a half hardy climber	10-May	15-Jun	36	>>>	39
Inula helenium	Elecampne	Large plant - also the same pretty much as Telekia	10-Jul	16-Aug	37	>>>>###**	99
Inula hookeri	Elecampne	Can be invasive but personally I have found it easy to control	10-Jul	10-Aug	31	>>>####**	98
Iris	Iris	Yellow Flag Iris and other non double Iris will be visited by bees, but are very short flowering	30-May	20-Jun	21	>>	20
Isatis tinctoria (N)	Woad	A UK wild flower. Biennial much liked by bees. Considered noxious weed in USA. Ok in a meadow, not really in a border	01-Jun	01-Jul	30	>>>*	48
Jasminum nudiflorum	Winter Jasmine	Nothing recorded where I am	20-Jan	20-Feb	31		0

Kalimeris	Asian or Korean Aster	Rarely grown, this is a good small perennial plant for all pollinators that may score more after review	17-Jul	10-Aug	24	>>#**	56
Kalmia latifolia	Kalmia	Acid soil shrub, bee unfriendly See the poisonous page	10-Jul	10-Aug		>>	20
Kerria	Jews Mallow	Avoid doubles such as "Pleniflora", "Golden Guinea" and "Variegata" have single flowers but plant produces mixed results	01-May	01-Jun	31	>>	28
Kirengeshoma palmata	Yellow Wax Bells	Needs acid soil, shade and careful nurturing, bumblebees visit sometimes	01-Jul	01-Aug	31	>>	28
Knautia avensis (N)	Field Scabious	Native wild flower, very good for insects. It is the food plant of the Marsh Fritillary, Bee Hawk Moth and a micro moth called Nemophora metallica	20-Jun	20-Jul	35	>>>####***	109
Knautia macedonica	Scabious	Will also flower later in Summer	25-May	27-Jul	63	>>>>####***	125
Kniphofia	Red Hot Poker	See article	20-May	15-Jun	28	>>>>*	57
Kolkwitzia	Beauty Bush	Is attractive to bees in May and June	15-May	10-Jun	26	>>>	37
Laburnhum watereri	Laburnham	Poisonous and planted less these days but is pollinated by bees. The negatives outweigh any positives	10-May	30-May	20	>>>	30
Lamiastrum galeobdolon	Dead Nettle	"Pink Chablis" is a good bee plant. The White Dead Nettle (N) also though briefer in flower	01-Apr	01-May	30	>>>*	48
Lathyrus latifolius	Everlasting Pea	Escaped from cottage gardens found in hedgerows. Perennial. Needs support	10-Jul	02-Sep	54	>>	34
Lathyrus pratensis	Meadow Vetchling	Food plant of butterfly for Wood White. Good meadow plant	05-May	18-May	13	>>~	30
Lavatera	Lavatera	All larger Lavatera are excellent wildlife plants. See article	15-Jun	05-Oct	112	>>>#***	98

Lavendula	Lavender	Lavender "Hidcote"/ Munstead	08-Jun	10-Jul	32	>>>>###**	98
Lavendula intermedia	Variety Sussex / Vera	Taller type with longer flowering period	15-Jul	15-Sep	62	>>>>####***	126
Layia platyglossa	Tidy Tips	Annual. Hot, Sunny position required	28-Jun	20-Aug	53	>>##**	73
Leonurus cardiaca	Motherwort	Rarely available herb with subtle flower and prickly seed heads	01-Aug	01-Sep	31	>>>**	58
Lespedeza	Bush Clover	Little response to this in UK	11-Sep	30-Sep	19	>	10
Leucanthemella	Hungarian Daisy	Late flowering perennial sometimes so late that everything else has finished…	20-Sep	10-Oct	20	>>**	40
Leucanthemum	Shasta Daisy	See article	12-Jul	20-Aug	39	**#	40
Leucanthemum (N)	Ox Eye Daisy	See article	03-May	10-Jun	38	>>>##**	80
Levisticum officinale	Lovage	Grows over 2 metres. Unremarkable flowers are attractive to many insects	01-Jul	01-Aug	31	>>*~	48
Leycesteria formosa	Pheasant Bush	See article	22-Jul	10-Oct	80	>>>##~	80
Liatris spicata	Blazing stars	Soft foliage is loved by slugs	20-Jul	02-Sep	44	>>>>**##	91
Ligularia	Leopard plant	All perennial species loved by slugs but "The Rocket" is more resilient	10-Jul	01-Aug	22	>>>**##	76
Ligustrum	Privet	Said by some to be a honey spoiler. Hedges pruned will not flower much. Unpruned plants flower sporadically and attract many insects	14-Jun	14-Jul	30	>>**~	58
Lilium martogan	Martogan Lily	The European native flower of alpine meadows is pollinated by bees. I would still be cautious regarding pets however	10-Jul	15-Aug	36	>>	29
Lamiastrum galeobdolan	Yellow archangel	Similar to Lamium with yellow flowers. Too invasive to plant, steer clear	15-Mar	10-Apr	26	>>>	47

Lillium	Lily	The main genus of perennial lilies can be fatal to cats. Poisonous to insects despite attracting them. Avoid	17-Jun	01-Aug	45	>>	31
Limnanthes douglasii	Poached Egg Plant	Annual. Needs many plants however	15-May	20-Jun	36	>>>***~	79
Limonium	Statis	Beloved by Flower Arrangers not by bees or butterflies	20-Jun	10-Jul	20		0
Linaria	Toadflax (N)	Very attractive to bees. Purple toadflax is best, (this is effectively a wild variety) in comparison to the pink version "Canon Went"	09-Jun	01-Aug	53	>>>>**#	83
Linaria repens	Creeping Toadflax	Likes gravel and walls. Rarely planted but a great bee plant	01-Jun	20-Aug	31	>>>***#	78
Liriodendron tulipifera	Tulip Tree	Too large for a small garden	27-Jun	15-Jul	18	>>	20
Lobelia siphilitica	Lobelia	Often sold as a water plant or bog plant slugs adore this. Having some attraction to bees	01-Aug	01-Oct	61	>>*	45
Lobelia erinus	Trailing Lobelia	For hanging baskets	01-Jul	01-Sep	62	>>*	46
Lobelia cardinalis	Lobelia		29-Jul	15-Oct	78	~>	40
Lobelia gerardii	Water Lobelia	Lovely plant but very prone to slug damage	25-Jul	15-Sep	52	>>>#	53
Lonicera fragrantissima	Winter Flowering Honeysuckle	As described by a friend, visited in Winter by bees in Croydon, Surrey	10-Jan	25-Feb	46	>>	32
Lonicera nitida	Hedging Honeysuckle	Yellow form "Baggesens Gold" is less invasive over time but still a beast	10-Apr	10-May	30	>>>	38
Lonicera periclymenum (N)	Honeysuckle	Attractive to Moths and not a troublesome plant, can grow up small trees without causing issues	20-Jun	20-Jul	30	>>###	58
Lotus corniculatus (N)	Birds Foot Trefoil	Small perennial. Best in a meadow	18-May	20-Jul	63	>>>##*	76
Lunaria (N)	Honesty	Biennial	02-Apr	27-May	55	>>##	54

Lupinus	Lupin	Attractive to slugs and aphids. Questions about bee interaction. Toxins said to reduce number of bumblebee offSpring so we should AVOID!	01-Jun	01-Jul	30	>>	28
Lupinus	Annual Lupins	See above	01-Jul	20-Jul	19	>>>	30
Lupinus arboreus	Tree Lupin	See above	02-Jun	10-Jul	38	>>>	40
Lychnis	Maltese Cross	Several varieties which are supposed to be attractive to butterflies. I scored nothing for the bright red "Maltese Cross" over many years. Ditto Lychnis coronaria	01-Jun	20-Jun	19		0
Lysimachia	Crimson Loosestrife	Lysimachia atropurpurea is maybe only a one year affair however it is relatively early in bloom and very good for bees in the border	20-May	05-Jul	46	>>>*#~	72
Lysimachia	Loosestrife	Lysimachia "Punctata" is commonly sold as a cheerful plant for shade. Lysimachia "Firecracker" is a dark brown leaved plant that performs better for insects	01-Jul	15-Aug	44	>>~	41
Lysimachia nummularia	Creeping Jenny	(N)	01-Jun	20-Jun	19	>	10
Lythrum salicaria	Purple Loosestrife	See article, one of the best plants for wildlife including (N) plant	20-Jul	01-Sep	43	>>>>####***	121
Macleya cordata	Plume Poppy	This monster plant 8 feet high with invasive tendancies would be worth a risk if it was a fabulous wildlife plant however I found little in terms of score for this	01-Jul	01-Sep	62	~	26
Magnolia Species	Magnolia	Not that attractive to insects	30-Apr	15-May	15		0
Mahonia	Mahonia	See article , Season Stretchers	20-Dec	16-Feb	58	>>~	45
Malva sylvestris	Mallow	See article on Malva	20-Jun	30-Jul	30	>>>>***	80

Marrubium vulgare	White Horehound	Favoured by some beekeepers. Easy small perennial plant for full sun with silver leaves and small flowers over a long period.	14-Jun	05-Aug	52	>>>**	63
Matricaria chamomilla (N)	Mayweed	Meadow plant similar to ox eye daisy. Good for small insects	20-May	15-Jul	56	>>*#	54
Matthiola	Stock	Little merit	01-Jun	01-Aug	61	>	25
Meconopsis cambrica	Welsh Poppy	(N) Native flower, may also flower in Autumn. Great for bumblebees	24-Apr	20-Aug	118	>>>>**~	100
Medicago sativa	Alfalfa	Normally grown as a crop	01-Jul	02-Aug	32	>>	28
Melissa	Bee Balm	Grow in a pot, invasive	01-Jun	01-Aug	61	>>>**	65
Melittis melissophyllum	Bastard Balm	Good cultivar of this small spreading plant is "Royal Velvet Distinction"	30-May	15-Aug	77	>>*	49
Mentha	Water Mint	Invasive (water) plant but good for bees and can still be used in cooking. Other mints get similar results	19-Jul	01-Sep	44	>>>##**	81
Mespilus germanica	Medlar	Bees are very keen on these flowers. Large Shrub or small tree	01-Jun	19-Jun	18	>>>	30
Mimulus	Monkey Flower	See article	25-Jul	30-Aug	36	>>>>	39
Monarda didyma	Bergamot	Simply a nightmare to keep slugs off, an excellent plant if you do for bees, "Cambridge Scarlet" is one of the best (red)	20-Jul	09-Sep	51	>>>	43
Muscari	Grape Hyacinth	Early flowering bulb with a little interest from insects	10-May	01-Jun	22	>~	26
Myrrhis odorata	Cicely	Herb which can get over 5 feet in height and self seeds. Tolerates some shade. Can be invasive!	25-Apr	25-Jun	61	>>**~	65
Myosotis sylvatica	Forget Me Knots	This is a comparitive study, so FMK do attract bees, but a Pulmonaria is much preferred	20-Apr	20-May	30	>#	28

Nandina domestica	Heavenly Bamboo	Variety "Firepower" has berries and flowers. May kill birds who eat too many Nandina berries due to an apparent content of cyanide within them.	01-Jun	20-Jun	19		0
Nanthesium ossifragum	Bog Asphodel	Wild bog flower like a small Asphodeline lutea	20-Jul	10-Aug	21	>~	20
Narcissus	Daffodil	Daffodils are said to be visited by very early emerging insects. However little visited various cultivated varieties I studied, and Crocus is a much better choice	20-Jan	10-Mar	49		0
Nectaroscordum siculicum	Sicilian Honey Garlic	Fantastic blooms for Bumblebees from a bulb	10-Jun	01-Jul	21	>>>>	40
Nemesia	Nemisia	Many types available and some are liked by bees, monitor at the garden centre. Half hardy	15-Jun	15-Aug	61	>>	35
Nepeta mussinii	Catmint	See article for "Six Hills Giant"	08-Jun	20-Jul	42	>>>>***~	91
Nicotiana	Tobacco Plant	Annual. For Bees and moths	01-Jul	01-Aug	31	>##	38
Nymphaea	Water lily	Beetles in the main like this	10-Jul	10-Aug	31	>#~	38
Oenothera	Evening Primrose	See article	16-Jun	10-Oct	116	>>###	79
Olearia	Daisy Bush	"Macrodonta" is an evergreen Tree with insect attracting white flowers and holly like leaves. "Hastii" to me was much less effective. Score is for "Macrodonta"	20-Aug	10-Sep	21	>>>**	50
Omphalodes	Navelwort		05-May	01-Jun	27	>	17
Onopordum acanthium	Scotch Thistle	A monster plant, however the area of flowers, versus the area the plant covers, is not great	19-Jul	15-Aug	27	>>>***##	87
Origanum	Marjoram	See article	05-Jul	06-Sep	63	>>>>####***	126
Ornithogalum	Star of Bethlehem	Bulb	01-Jul	20-Jul	19	>>	20
Osmanthus	Tea Olive	Evergreen bush	06-Jul	15-Aug	40	>>	30

Osteospernum	Osteospernum	"Blackthorn seedling" is most hardy of the varieties. Most will not get through a hard Winter. There are better plants	20-Jun	30-Aug	71	>>	38
Oxalis	Sorrel	Do not plant this, it is invasive	01-Jun	01-Jul	30	>#	28
Pachysandra terminalis	Pachysandra	Ground cover plant with early flowers. Contains toxic alkaloids	01-Apr	20-Apr	19		0
Paeonia lactiflora	Peony "White Wings"	There is much to reward insects during the blooming of this single, white Peony	08-May	01-Jun	24	>>>**	56
Papaver	Large Flowered Poppies	All are brief in flower	03-Jun	20-Jun	17	>>>*~	50
Papaver nudicaule	Iceland Poppy	Slug Damage is a problem	10-May	20-Jun	41	>>	30
Papaver rhoeas (N)	red poppy	The Flanders poppy is pollinated mostly by bees	10-Jun	10-Jul	30	>>>	38
Papaver somniferum	Opium Poppy	So brief in flower!	10-Jun	20-Jun	10	>>>	30
Parahebe	Parahebe	Attractive to Bees in garden centres. "Kenty Pink" and "Avalanche" are noted	04-May	10-Jul	67	>>	37
Passiflora caerulea	Passion Flower	Exotic looking climber to grow up a sunny wall in well drained soil in the South and Midlands of the UK Can be large 4x4 metres. Bees like the flowers , more will appear in a good hot Summer	01-Jul	30-Jul	29	>>#	37
Pastinaca sativa	Wild Parsnip	Good plant for wildlife but horrible for humans in terms of potential skin irritation / burns from touching the plant, if you then expose skin to sun	14-Jul	10-Aug	27	>>***	57
Penstemon	Penstemon	See article	20-Jun	10-Sep	82	>>>>**#	91
Perovskia	Russian Sage		10-Aug	10-Oct	61	>>*	45
Persicaria	Amphibious bistort	Visited by bees	10-Jun	25-Jun	15	>>	20
Persicaria	Bistort (N)	See article	25-Apr	20-May	25	>>>*~~	66

Persicaria	Knotweed	See article	15-Jul	15-Sep	62	>>>**~~~	96
Persicaria polymorpha	Persicaria	This attracts little	09-Jun	20-Jul	41		0
Petunia (species)	Petunia	Popular as a plant, but useless for insects	01-Jul	01-Oct			0
Petasites fragrans	Winter Heliotrope	This flowers in mid Winter from November to Feb. Invasive	30-Dec	18-Feb	50	>	23
Petasites hybridus (N)	Butterbur	Unusual plant of damp riverside, flowers appear first, then massive leaves .Not suitable for gardens but good in the wild	01-Apr	25-Jun	85	>>>*#	71
Phacelia tanacetifolia	Fiddleneck	Annual	01-Jul	18-Aug	48	>>>##~*	82
Philadelphus	Mock Orange	Single flowers only. Large Shrub	25-Jun	15-Jul	20	>>>#	40
Phlomis fruiticosa	Jerusalem Sage	Other plants are much preferred	20-May	20-Jun	31	>>	28
Phlox paniculata	Phlox	Butterflies and Moths love it. Other reference books say bees like it. They don't. Best variety is the purple "Neon Purple" and white "White Admiral" But the light purple plant from my mums garden, 40 years in cultivation, is the longest flowering	30-Jun	26-Sep	88	####~	72
Phormium tenax	Phormium	Huge perennial . A case of something too exotic for the UK. Mostly planted for foliage and our local bees will find flowers, when found, difficult	20-Jul	20-Aug	30	>	19
Photinia	Photinia	The type known as "Red Robin" has the ability to bloom with great benefit to insects, though you will not want to prune the plant, to get that effect	25-May	20-Jun	26	>>>**	57
Phygelius	Cape fushcia	Is visited by bees, the plant performs better in urban areas	01-Jul	10-Aug	40	>>	30
Physalis	Chinese Lantern	The lanterns are prominent but the flowers less so.	01-Jul	20-Jul	19	**	20

Physocarpus	Ninebark	See article	20-May	15-Jun	26	>>>**	57
Physostegia	Obedient Plant		20-Jul	20-Aug	31	>>#	38
Pieris japonica	Pieres	Acid soil shrub. This is said to taint honey - one subject to further review	01-May	01-Jun	31	>>>	38
Pileostegia viburnoides	Climbing Hydrangea	See article	15-Aug	06-Oct	52	>>>>**	73
Pittosporum tenuifolium	Pittispurnum	See article	20-May	18-Jun	29	>>~~	57
Platycodon grandifloras	Balloon Flower	Campanula varieties as stated are better than this plant.	03-Jul	29-Jul	26	>>	27
Polemonium caeruleum	Jacobs Ladder	Often sold as good for bees this plant is flowering for a short time only and only briefly of interest	20-May	15-Jun	26	>>#	37
Polygonatum	Solomons Seal (N)	Solomons Seal Sawfly will normally eat all the leaves at some point	01-May	20-May	19	>>~~	40
Pontederia cordata	Pickerel Weed	Pond plant with blue flowers	10-Jul	25-Sep	77	>>#	49
Potentilla fruiticosa	Shrubby Cinquefoil	See article	07-Jul	15-Oct	100	>>>***##~	115
Potentilla anserina	Silverweed Potentila	Available in garden centres in yellow red and pink, this plant has a short flowering period	20-May	20-Jun	31	>	18
Primula	Candlelabra Primula	Limited in responses	08-May	26-Jun	49	>~	32
Primula vulgaris (N)	Vulgaris	Primrose, flowers around "Primrose Day" in April. Best hope is for a passing Brimstone to visit. Food plant for the Duke of Burgundy Fritillary	03-Apr	29-May	56	>##	44
Primula veris (N)	Cowslips	Wild flower food plant of the Duke of Burgundy Fritillary Butterfly, Plain Clay & Northern Rustic Moth	31-Mar	05-May	35	>>>#	49
Prostanthera	Mint Bush	Australian plant of which even the most hardy of larger leaved forms won't get through a UK Winter	07-Jun	10-Jul	33	>>*	38

Prunella (N)	Selfheal	Native which sporadically can be very attractive to bees	06-Jun	10-Aug	65	>>#*	56
Prunus	Cherry Plum	Single flowers only	25-Mar	10-Apr	16	>>>	30
Prunus dulcis	Almond Tree	Open flowers do attract most bees	25-Apr	25-May	30	>>>	38
Prunus laurocerasus	Cherry Laurel	Leaves produce cyanide gas that can kill an insect. Plant is invasive, too large and may taint honey. I'm not sure I like the atmosphere it creates	24-Apr	15-Jun	52	>>>	43
Prunus spinosa (N)	Blackthorn	Native	20-Mar	20-Apr	31	>>##	48
Pulicaria dysenterica (N)	Fleabane	Water meadow plant needs acid soil no chalk. Perennial to 1 metre which grows in a variety of habitats from water meadows to the drive outside my front door	05-Aug	10-Sep	36	>>>**##~~	99
Pulmonaria	Lungwort	See article, the best early Spring flower for insects	20-Feb	25-Apr	64	>>>>*~	76
Pulsatilla	Pasqueflower	Flowers early in the year, great for emerging bumblebees. The flowers are notoriously brief	10-Mar	25-Mar	15	>>>	30
Pyracantha	Pyracantha	Prickly plant provides good berries for birds, good flowers for bees	10-Jun	28-Jun	18	>>>#**	60
Ranunculus (N)	Buttercup sp	A study (C Sedivy et al) suggests bees are not poisoning larvae by feeding them buttercup pollen. However anecdotal evidence contradicts this. With buttercups being so common, would we not know of a problem with honey bees by now? Otherwise invasive plant	16-May	20-Jun	35	>**~	49
Rehmannia elata	Chinese Foxglove	Often seen in garden centres, these will not always get through a normal UK Winter, though you can grow it in a large pot or protect it and it may do ok	26-Jun	10-Sep	76	>>>	49
Reseda lutea (N)	Weld	Plant in a hot dry position. Very good for solitary bee types and unassuming, plants can bloom for a long time	30-Jun	05-Sep	67	>>**	57

Reseda odorata (N)	Mignonette	Attracts wide range of insects recommended as long ago as 1876!	30-Jun	20-Sep	82	>>>~*	71
Rheum palmatum	Cultivated Rhubarb	Large perennial. Not especially attractive to insects. Bad ratio of plant size to bloom size	30-Jun	30-Jul	30	>	18
Rhododenron	Rhododenron	Negative plant for honey bees and some other species. Causes death and contaminates honey. Rhododenron ponticum is a chief culprit. Bumblebees feed without being harmed	05-May	10-Jun	36	>>>	39
Rhus typhina	Stags Horn Sumach	Invasive plant though undeniable fantastic foliage and good insect plant. Don't be tempted though…	05-Jun	30-Jun	25	>>>*#	56
Ribes	Flowering Currant	See article	25-Mar	25-Apr	30	>>>	38
Ricinus	Castor Oil Plant	Seeds are very poisonous and plant is toxic to the honey bee. Score is irrelevant. This plant is used to produce bio-diesel so our demand for fuel could kill many bees					0
Robinia	Honey Locust	Too big for the small garden and flowers erratically. Flowers are attractive to bees it produces honey in warmer climates than the UK	10-Jun	30-Jun	20	>>>	30
Rodgersia	Rodgersia	A large plant often found in marshy areas and shade. Other choices are better than this	01-Jul	01-Aug	31	>	18
Romneya coulteri	Tree or Matilija Poppy	Where it likes growing it is invasive, taller than you and probably best away from a house. It needs fussing to succeed, best left to gardeners with lots of time, room, or luck	02-Jul	20-Sep	80	>>>**~	80
Rosa	Rose	See article					
Rosa rugosa	Wild Rose	Also includes Rosa arvensis Good for bees but too much of a prickly monster for a small garden	10-Jun	30-Jun	20	>>>**#	60

Rosmarinus officinalis	Rosemary	Buy in flower as some varieties are shy flowering. This score is for a good plant	30-Mar	30-Apr	31	>>>#	48
Rubus fruiticosa	Bramble	Unsuitable for gardens though blooms are loved by most insects. Invasive	05-Jul	30-Jul	25	>>>**#~	76
Rudbeckia	Goldsturm	I don't see much interest in the smaller Rudbeckias. Insects pass this by for plants such as Caryopteris	20-Jul	05-Oct	77	>>	39
Ruscus aculeatus	Butchers Broom	Spikey sub shrub with small flowers that are pollinated by insects. Considered a wild flower in dry places and dunes. Makes a good broom if foliage is collected together	10-Jun	10-Jul	30	>~	28
Ruta graveolens	Rue	Avoid! Can be damaging to skin if comes into contact with you!	01-Jul	01-Aug	31	>>	28
Salix caprea	Pussy Willow	"Kilmarnock"	01-Mar	25-Mar	20	>>>*~	50
Salvia jamensis	Sage	See article	20-Jun	19-Aug	60	>>**	55
Salvia nemorosa	Sage (Perennial)	See article	10-Jun	20-Jul	40	>>>**	60
Sambucus nigra (N)	Elder	Don't eat berries. Bees found other things they prefer than this plant	20-Jun	15-Jul	25	~	16
Sambucus racemosa	Cut Leaved Elder	Slightly better than Nigra, flies and some bees like it	30-Apr	15-May	15	>>~~	40
Sanguisorba	Burnet	Tenuifolia rather than the wild flower is sold as being good for bees and butterflies. Not for me though	30-Apr	20-May	20	~~	20
Sanicula europaea	Sanicle	Short lived flower herb	23-May	01-Aug	70	>	28
Santolina	Cotton Lavender	A plant of dry places, with button yellow flowers that appear in Summer, it is not a plant that attracts very much	20-Jun	20-Jul	30	>	18
Sanvitalia	Creeping Zinnia	This would be great for a hanging basket as it attracts bees and hoverflies	01-Jul	01-Sep	62	>>**	56

Saponaria	Soapwort	Sold as a good bee plant, there are double forms that do not work, and look unattractive and single forms that are invasive. I would avoid this plant	20-Jul	20-Sep	62	>>*	46
Saxifraga x urbium	London Pride	The form called "London Pride" is liked by hoverflies. (Saxifraga x urbium)	20-Apr	20-May	30	>~~	38
Scabiosa columbaria	Scabious	"Butterfly Blue" is a good selection see article	15-May	01-Aug	78	###>>>*	90
Schizostylis	Kaffir Lily		10-Sep	15-Oct	35	~	19
Scilla	Squill	Scilla siberica is a small bulbous Spring plant liked by early bees	10-Apr	20-May	40	>>>	40
Scutellaria	Skullcap	See article	10-May	20-Jun	41	>>>>	50
Sedum	Stonecrop	"Purple Emperor"	14-Jun	10-Jul	26	>>>~	47
Sedum	Biting Stonecrop	Often found on green roofs	10-Jun	25-Jun	15	>>*	30
Sedum	Ice Plant	See article. "Matrona Telephium"	10-Sep	10-Oct	30	>>>###*	78
Selinum	Selinum	Like a cow parsley plant	10-Jul	01-Aug	22	>*~	36
Senecio greyi	Now Brachyglottis	Often found in car parks, this was once everywhere. Too short a flowering period to be useful	27-Jun	20-Jul	23	>*#	36
Sidalcea	Mallow	The flowers are smaller than Lavatera, and it should be a good bee plant, I have not found it that easy to grow	15-Jun	15-Jul	30	>>	28
Silene dioica (N)	Red Campion	See article,	15-May	10-Jun	26	>>>*#	57
Silene vulgaris (N)	Bladder Campion	Wildflower is of use to hover flies and flies and night time moths	15-Jun	29-Jun	14	*#~	30
Silphium laciniatum	Compass Plant	See article	18-Jul	20-Aug	33	>>>**##~~	98

Sinacalia tangutica	Chinese Groundsel	Flowers are Like Ligularia - needs to be contained. Scarcely garden worthy, Golden Rod is more attractive!	01-Jul	20-Jul	19	>>>**	50
Sinapis alba	White Mustard	Annual plant	20-May	20-Jul	61	>>##	55
Sisyrinchium	Blue Eyed Grass		10-Jun	05-Jul	25	>>	26
Skimmia	Skimmia japonica	Only certain varieties are attractive to bees of which "Rubella" is one	01-Apr	01-May	30	>>>	38
Smilacina	False Spikeard	No significant result	10-Jun	20-Jun	10	>	10
Solanum crispum	Climbing Potato	Climbing plant	01-May	01-Jul	61	>>*	45
Solidago canadensis	Golden Rod	This plant is very attractive to a wide range of insect life	20-Jul	31-Aug	42	>>##**~~	101
Sophora japonica	Sophora	The Pagoda tree is recommended by bee keepers but to wait 30 years for flowers is a stretch!!	01-Aug	02-Sep	32	>>>	38
Sophora microphylla "Sun King"	Sophora "Sun King"	As long ago as 1971 this plant was identified as causing death to bees, yet it is still sold as being a wildlife friendly plant	10-Mar	15-Apr	36	>>>*	49
Sorbaria arborea	Sorbaria	See article. It is a brilliant plant for all insects	01-Jul	10-Aug	40	>>>>##~~	100
Sorbus aria (N)	Whitebeam		15-May	30-May	15	>	10
Sorbus aucuparia (N)	Rowan		04-May	15-May	11	>>~	30
Sorbus hupehensis	Chinese Rowan		15-May	01-Jun	17	>>>**	50
Spartium	Spanish Broom	I spent many years seeing no bees on this plant, despite its potential	01-Jul	15-Jul	14		0
Spiraea	Spiraea "Gold Mound"		05-May	05-Jun	31	>>	28
Spiraea japonicum	Spiraea "Anthony Waterer"	See article, the best of the Spiraea plants available	01-Jul	20-Aug	50	>>##**	73
Spiraea japonicum	Spiraea "Genpei"		01-Jul	20-Aug	50	>>**	53

Stachys lanata	Lambs Ears	Wool Carder bee will use the hairy leaves for its nest. Avoid foliage only plants such as "Big Ears" the best variety for flowers is just the standard Stachys lanata. If in doubt buy in flower at the garden centre. Must be grown in a sunny position for success	20-Jun	30-Jul	40	>>>*	50
Stachys macrantha	Betony	Officianalis is the wild plant	01-Jun	29-Jun	28	>	17
Stachys sylvatica	Hedge woundwort	Food plant of Garden Tiger, Small Rivulet moth	15-May	20-Jun	36	>>#*	49
Stellaria	Chickweed		20-Jun	20-Jul	30	>*~	38
Stokesia	Stokesia	Needs well drained soil in Sun	05-Jun	20-Jul	45	>>**#	61
Symphoricarpus alba	Snowberry	Tolerates shade even deep shade. Invasive suckering shrub. related to Campanula	25-Jun	01-Sep	36	>>>#	57
Symphytum alba	Comfrey	See article	15-Apr	10-Jun	56	>>>*	54
Symphytum	Wild Comfrey	Too coarse to be planted in anything except a very wild garden	01-Jun	10-Jul	39	>>>	40
Syringa	Lilac	Yes butterflies like it, but very few are about this early	20-Apr	05-May	15	##	20
Tagetes	Marigold	Slugs like this plant too	20-Jun	10-Sep	82	>>**	61
Tanacetum coccineum	Pyrethrum	This plant is the basis of insecticide. It just feels wrong to me to plant this!	10-Jun	20-Jul	40	>>*	40
Tanacetum parthenium	Feverfew	Ladybirds like it, it is not attractive to insects otherwise	15-Jun	20-Aug	66	~~	37
Tanacetum vulgare	Tansy	Avalable on yellow and a white form. A good insect plant	20-May	10-Jul	51	>>>**##	83
Telekia speciosa	Telekia	Very like Elecampne and also good for bees and butterflies a very large plant	15-Jun	20-Jul	35	>>**##	69
Teucrium hircanicum	Germander	See article on Teucrium Species. Excellent plant	10-Jul	20-Aug	41	>>>>**###	100
Thalictrum aquilegiifolium	Meadow Rue	See Article	25-May	20-Jun	26	>>>**	57

Thalictrum delavayi	Meadow Rue	Little response to this	30-Jul	20-Aug	21	>	10
Thalictrum flavum	Meadow Rue	Yellow / Creamy coloured vareity very popular with bees	28-May	02-Jul	35	>>>#**~	79
Thermopsis	False Lupin	Do not move once planted	20-Jun	15-Jul	25	>>>	36
Thymus	Thyme	Thyme See Article	20-May	01-Jul	42	>>>##**	81
Tiarella cordifolia	Foam Flower	Heuchera, a related plant, is visited more	20-May	15-Jun	26	>>*	37
Tithonia	Mexican Sunflower	Large, space using annual	25-Jul	02-Sep	39	>>**##	70
Tradescantia	Spiderwort	Loved by slugs	20-May	15-Jun	26	>>*	37
Tropaeolum majus	Nasturtium	Annual	02-Jul	10-Sep	70	>>>	48
Trifolium	Clover	White and Red Clover are very good for bees in a wildlife meadow situation Be careful not to walk on the lawn when in flower as bees will be low level - don't squash them!	25-Jun	25-Jul	30	>>>**#	73
Trillium	Wake Robin	Will be attacked by slugs Prefers acid soil and shade	05-May	30-May	25	>>	26
Tripleurospermum	Scentless Mayweed	Large ironically smelly white daisy flower of waste ground	10-Jun	01-Jul	21	>**~	40
Trollius europaeus	Globeflower	Early flowering	15-May	25-Jun	41	>~~	40
Tulipa	Tulip	Many different types of plants and the single flower should be attractive but mainly isn't	25-Feb	20-Apr	54	>	24
Typha latifolia (N)	Reed Mace	See Article	01-Jul	01-Aug	50	~	23
Ulex europaeus	Gorse	Too vicious with its spines!	20-Feb	29-May	99	>>*#	75
Uvularia Grandiflora	Merrybells	Liked by bees, slugs, deer, seek advice on growing	10-Apr	30-Apr	20	>>*	30
Vaccinium species	Bilberry/ Cowberry	Acid loving plants, excellent for bees even having a "Bilberry Bee" that specialises	01-Jun	01-Jul	30	>>>*	48

198

Valerian officianalis	Common Valerian	Preferable to red valerian as easier to control. Large	04-Jun	25-Jun	21	>>>###**	80
Veratrum	False Hellebore	Difficult to grow and rarely is available—does not attract insects but will kill those that visit. Score irrelevant					
Verbascum olympicum	Giant Mullein	Large Biennial	28-Jun	01-Oct	95	>>*#	64
Verbena bonariensis	Purple Top	Great plant! Also Goldfinches and other birds love the seeds when left on the plant	15-Jul	20-Oct	97	***####>>>>~	144
Veronica		Veronica spicata (blue) and various pink forms including "Foxy" are good	20-Jun	20-Aug	61	>>>	45
Veronicastrum	Culvers Root	Love this plant which is like a very large veronica. Spires of flowers, very attractive to bees	25-Jun	01-Sep	68	>>>>**#	87
Viburnham	Viburnham	Tinus	02-Feb	02-Apr	59	>	94
Viburnham opulus	Viburnham	Poisonous berries are good for birds	20-May	10-Jun		>#~	30
Viburnum rhytidophyllum	Viburnham	Large Shrub, brief in flower	20-Apr	15-May	25	>	16
Vicia cracca	Tufted Vetch	Bird Vetch and other Vetches are good for meadowland	10-Jun	10-Jul	30	>>	28
Vinca	Great Periwinkle	Takes over a huge section of garden, with little benefit to wildlife	01-Apr	20-Apr	19		0
Viola tricolor (N)	Wild Pansy	AKA Heartsease. Charming wild flower which offers much more than any cultivated "Pansy"	20-May	20-Jun	31	>>**#	58
Waldsteinia ternata	Waldsteinia	Good groundcover plant	20-May	20-Jun	31	>>*	38
Watsonia		Did not record any results	15-Aug	09-Sep	25		
Weigela	Weigela	"Bristol Ruby" is best variety	20-May	01-Jul	42	>>>*~	61
Yucca	Yucca	Bees like it but you won't when you have to cut back this spiny viscious plant	01-Jul	01-Aug	31	>>	28

Zantedeschia	Calla Lily		06-Jul	25-Jul	19	>>~~	40
Zinnia peruviana	Zinnia	Pick single flowered ones only. Half hardy annual. Do not move the plant	10-Jul	10-Aug	31	>>*#	48

Dictionary of Terms

Acid and Alkaline – Soil types. Plants have evolved to a very wide range of conditions and many that grow on Alkaline soil with a high PH value will not grow on Acid soil.

Annual – Plant that flowers and produces seed in one year and may not come back the next unless seeds germinate the next year.

Base – applied to foliage, the leaves close to the ground.

Biennial – Plant that forms a rosette the first year and flowers and produces seed in the second year.

Bulb – Plant that grows from a potato like structure that contains all the energy to grow.

Canker – Bacterial disease of Trees usually with symptoms of oozing clear or brown liquid from wounds in the bark.

Ericaceous compost – sold in garden centres this is for plants that do not tolerate soil that contains lime or is alkaline

Food Chain – Insects are at the bottom of the food chain. They are eaten by birds. Birds are eaten by Mammals or other Birds of Prey. So the Mammals are at the top of the food chain.

Forage – The act of looking for a food source (pollen and nectar for insects) from plants.

Half Hardy – Plant that may get killed by frost or iced conditions.

Hardy – Plant that will get through most Winters.

Nutrients – elements within the soil that help a plant grow. Some plants like a lot, others prefer less nutritious soil, such as some meadow plants.

Perennial – Plant that comes back from soil level each year having died back in Autumn.

Photosynthesis – the chemical reaction which occurs in leaves of plants that converts light into energy for the plants.

Pollinating Insects – Any insect that visits a flower can pollinate or fertilise it. However this expression is usually reserved for all types of bee, hoverflies, butterflies and moths.

Preference – Applied to foraging insects, the favourite plant which is preferred to others.

Pupa/Chrysalis – the life stage between immature and mature, a dry package containing a transforming insect.

Umbels – Fennel has flowers on widely separated stalks this pattern also seen on flowers like cow parsley is described as umbels.

Well drained – soil that contains grit, so that moisture does not stay around the plant.

Further Recommended Reading

BUMBLEBEES AN INTRODUCTION
DR NIKKI GAMMANS AND OTHERS
BUMBLEBEE CONSERVATION TRUST
The best identification book available that has drawings and photos of Bumblebees

THE GARDEN JUNGLE – DAVE GOULSON
CAPE PUBLISHING
Dave writes inspiring text about how to make your garden more ecologically valuable

BUTTERFLY GARDENING – JENNY STEEL
BRAMBLEBYBOOKS

DANCING WITH BEES – BRIGIT STRAWBRIDGE HOWARD 2019 – *CHELSEA GREEN*
A charming book, a journey back to nature and bees

WILD FLOWERS – NEIL FLETCHER
DORLING KINDERSLEY

INSECTS AND FLOWERS – JOHN BRACKENBURY *BLANDFORD*

TREES OF THE COUNTRYSIDE – FAIRHURST SOOTHILL *BLANDFORD*
The last two are long out of print classics that are worth getting hold of for the unique information they contain

About the Author

Michael Seabrook was formulating his research into insects for many years whilst working as an Insurance Underwriter.

When his career unfortunately paused in 2018 he started to compile all the information recorded into this book.

Michael is single, lives in Surrey, UK and is available as a Biodiversity Consultant and Wildlife Garden Designer. He is also a musician, pianist and composer. He releases electronic music on behalf of the artist Maxx Silver who can be found on You Tube and elsewhere

He loves visiting Italy, spending time with friends and tending to his wildlife garden.

Lightning Source UK Ltd.
Milton Keynes UK
UKHW051846020720
365931UK00004B/146